HOW TO MEASURE CUSTOMER SATISFACTION

Nigel Hill, John Brierley and Rob MacDougall

Gower

Published by
Gower Publishing Limited
Gower House
Croft Road
Aldershot
Hampshire GU11 3HR
England

Gower
Old Post Road
Brookfield
Vermont 05036
USA

Nigel Hill, John Brierley and Rob MacDougall have asserted their right under the Copyright, Designs and Patents Act 1988 to be identified as the authors of this work.

British Library Cataloguing in Publication Data
Hill, Nigel
   How to measure customer satisfaction
   1. Consumer satisfaction – Research   2. Consumer satisfaction
   – Evaluation   3. Market surveys
   I. Title   II. Brierley, John   III. MacDougall, Rob

ISBN 0 566 08193 8

Library of Congress Cataloging-in-Publication Data
Hill, Nigel, 1952–
   How to measure customer satisfaction / Nigel Hill, John Brierley
   and Rob MacDougall.
      p.   cm.
   ISBN 0-566-08193-8 (pbk.)
   1. Consumer satisfaction–Evaluation.   I. Brierley, John.
   II. MacDougall, Rob.   III. Title.
   HF5415.335.H553   1999
   658.8'12–dc21
                                                           98–53694
                                                           CIP

Typeset in Plantin Light by IML Typographers, Chester and printed in Great Britain by MPG Books Ltd, Bodmin

CONTENTS

LIST OF FIGURES

1 INTRODUCTION

Customer satisfaction measurement (CSM from now on) is a mature discipline in North America, but in the UK and other English-speaking countries it is still only at the early adopter stage and many other developed economies lag even further behind. We're no longer so arrogant that we expect customers to fit in with us and do business with us on our terms. Most UK organisations do now understand that it's up to the supplier to meet the needs of its customers if it wants to keep them. Indeed, in a recent survey of chief executives five out of every six claimed that improving customer satisfaction was one of the top priorities of their organisation. But then what do they do? Forty per cent do absolutely nothing to monitor whether or not they're achieving that objective, and a further third do so only by reviewing customer complaints – even though most of them probably do know that formal complaints are usually only the tip of the dissatisfaction iceberg. That leaves just over one quarter who use more systematic methods. These may include internal quality-of-service monitors, mystery customer programmes and customer satisfaction surveys. Internal monitoring of service standards and mystery shopping are both very useful sources of information, but the ultimate arbiters of customer satisfaction must be the customers themselves. A reliable method of listening to the 'voice of the customer' is therefore essential. Unfortunately, many customer surveys currently carried out by companies provide a far from reliable indication of customer satisfaction.

This book provides a step-by-step guide to the professional methods used to generate reliable measures of customer satisfaction. However, for the large majority of organisations which still have no formal system for listening to the voice of the customer and monitoring satisfaction, what's the point of doing it at all?

Why is customer satisfaction measured?

Competitiveness and profitability are maximised in the long run by *doing best what matters most to customers*. A CSM programme will therefore enable you to:

- Understand how customers perceive your organisation and whether your performance meets their expectations.
- Identify PFIs (priorities for improvement) – areas where improvements in performance will produce the greatest gain in customer satisfaction.
- Undertake a cost–benefit analysis to assess the overall business impact of addressing the PFIs.
- Pinpoint 'understanding gaps' where your own staff have a misunderstanding of customers' priorities or their ability to meet customers' needs.
- Set goals for service improvement and monitor progress against a customer satisfaction index.
- Benchmark your performance against that of other organisations.
- Increase profits through improved customer loyalty and retention.

There is growing evidence of the link which we all intuitively know to exist between customer satisfaction, loyalty and profitability. In the USA, where CSM is more mature and companies have several years of trend data, many have developed 'business performance models' (see Figure 1.1), enabling them to forecast financial performance from shifts in their CSM data. Some can even take the model back as far as employee satisfaction.

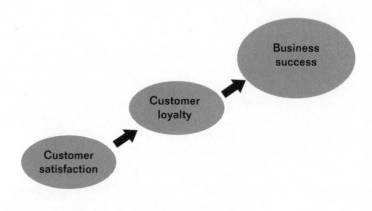

Figure 1.1 Business performance modelling

Not surprisingly, many companies have discovered that there is a strong correlation between satisfaction and loyalty only at the highest levels of customer satisfaction. Figure 1.2, based on data from companies such as AT&T, Rank Xerox and The Royal Bank of Scotland, shows that, on average, 95 per cent of customers scoring 'excellent' or 'very satisfied' (ticking the top box) subsequently remain loyal compared with only 65 per cent who score 'good' or 'satisfied'. As might be expected, the loyalty rate then plummets even more dramatically to 15 per cent for 'average' or the middle box, only 2 per cent for 'poor' or 'quite dissatisfied', and no future loyalty at all for those scoring in the bottom box. This explains why many organisations which are experienced in CSM say that only 'top-box' scores can be regarded as an acceptable level of performance.

Customer's stated level of satisfaction	Loyalty rate
Excellent/very satisfied	95%
Good/satisfied	65%
Average/neither satisfied nor dissatisfied	15%
Poor/quite dissatisfied	2%
Very poor/very dissatisfied	0%

Figure 1.2   Satisfaction–loyalty links

Satisfaction, loyalty and delight

Some people have suggested in recent times that customer satisfaction is 'old hat' and that we should be concentrating on customer loyalty and 'delighting the customer' (see Figure 1.3). Usually people making such statements can give no distinctive definitions of the three concepts and certainly no explanation of the causal effects.

Other people have claimed that CSM programmes have 'failed to deliver the goods' in their organisation. Hardly surprising. A CSM survey can deliver very accurate data on customers' level of satisfaction and can highlight the areas where customers are least happy but it can't solve the problems, improve the service and increase customer satisfaction. That relies on decisions, action and a lot of hard work. In our experience we have seen a huge gulf between the most and least customer-focused organisations both in terms of their speed of reaction to CSM results and the effectiveness of actions taken. If a CSM programme does fail it is very rarely the information that's the problem, but the organisation's inability to turn it into effective action afterwards.

Figure 1.3 Keeping customers – some concepts

An overview of the CSM process

This book will explain how to produce reliable measures of customer satisfaction and what needs to be done if those measures are to be successfully used as the basis for effective action. We will also return to the concepts of satisfaction, loyalty and delight in the final chapter and dispel a few myths about their relative contributions. But first, an overview of the CSM process (see Figure 1.4).

The starting point for any project is to set objectives and plan a detailed critical path for the exercise, and these will be covered in Chapter 2. The first stage of the research proper is to clarify with customers exactly what their requirements are so that an appropriate questionnaire, which asks the right questions, can be designed. This is done through exploratory research using focus groups (typically in consumer markets) or one-to-one depth interviews (the norm in business markets). It is customers' most important requirements, as stated by the customers themselves, that must form the basis for a CSM questionnaire and not assumptions you make in-house about what you think might be important to customers. The exploratory research process is covered in Chapter 3.

Two main factors determine the accuracy of a CSM study. The first is asking the right questions (hence the exploratory research); the second is asking them of the right people – a sample of customers that accurately reflects your customer base. Three things decide the accuracy of a sample. It must be representative, it must be randomly selected and it must be large enough. In Chapter 4 we examine the various sampling options.

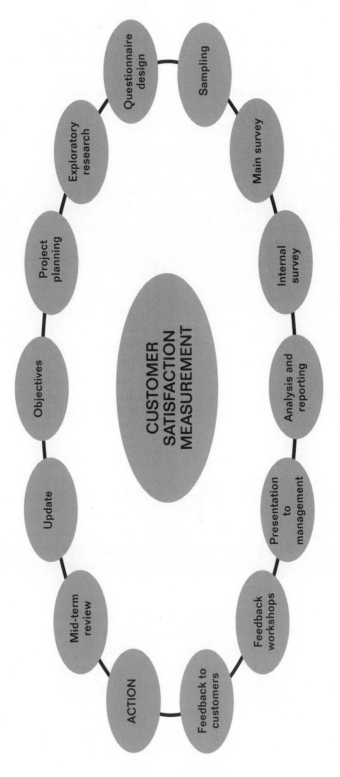

Figure 1.4 An overview of the CSM process

Once you are confident that you will be asking the right questions of the right people, you can design the final questionnaire and begin the main survey. The first decision here is to determine how the survey will be carried out. It could be done using telephone interviews, personal interviews or self-completion questionnaires, and the last can come in a number of forms, including postal, point of sale and electronic. Chapter 5 outlines the survey options, together with their advantages and disadvantages. Whatever survey type you adopt, it will be important to maximise response rates and this topic is covered in Chapter 6.

Having determined the type of survey you will carry out, you can design an appropriate questionnaire. Chapter 7 will examine general questionnaire design principles, whilst Chapter 8 will focus on the specific issue of rating scales. Even now one more step is necessary before launching into the survey. It must be properly introduced to customers. How this should be done is outlined in Chapter 9.

At this point the survey can finally be carried out, followed swiftly by an analysis of the results. Chapter 10 examines several analytical techniques and highlights some common mistakes to avoid. We also explain how to calculate an accurate customer satisfaction index. Once you have produced a set of results and established a satisfaction index, it is useful to know how your performance compares with that achieved by other organisations. Chapter 11 therefore covers the subject of satisfaction benchmarking.

A worthwhile addition to a CSM study is an internal survey where the same set of questions is administered to your own employees to discover whether they understand what's important to customers and how closely they are meeting customers' requirements. Typically conducted using self-completion questionnaires, an internal survey will often trace the origin of customer satisfaction problems to employees' inaccurate understanding of the customer perspective – the so-called 'understanding gaps'. Chapter 12 explains how to conduct and analyse an internal survey.

After analysing the data and producing a report, you should provide prompt feedback to employees and customers. Inadequate feedback is a common reason why some organisations fail to reap the full rewards of their CSM process. Only if employees fully understand the survey results and their implications will effective action be taken. Chapter 13 suggests how effective internal and external feedback can be provided.

The final chapter will return to those basic concepts of satisfaction, delight and loyalty to clarify the relationships and recommend the key areas to focus on for an effective CSM process in your organisation.

2 SETTING OBJECTIVES AND PROJECT PLANNING

Definition

If you want to measure customer satisfaction you need a very clear definition of exactly what you are measuring. Luckily, understanding the concept of customer satisfaction is easy. All you have to do is think how you feel when you're a customer – in the supermarket, on the train, having your car serviced – anywhere. Satisfaction is simple. If you get what you wanted, if your requirements are met, you are satisfied. If they're not met, you will not be satisfied. That simple definition (shown in Figure 2.1), tells us something fundamental about customer satisfaction – it's not an absolute concept; it's a relative one. It's relative to what the customer expected in the first place. So to measure satisfaction you have to measure both sides of that equation – the expectation part, usually called importance ratings, and the satisfaction part, usually called satisfaction ratings, but sometimes referred to as performance ratings.

> **Customer satisfaction is a measure of how your organisation's 'total product' performs in relation to a set of customer requirements**

Figure 2.1 Customer satisfaction – a definition

Objectives

1 Customers' requirements (importance ratings)
2 Customer satisfaction (satisfaction ratings)
3 Comparisons with other organisations
4 PFIs (priorities for improvement)
5 Customer satisfaction index
6 A trackable measure of satisfaction
7 The internal perspective

Figure 2.2 CSM objectives

The starting point for a CSM project must be to set objectives. There are several generic objectives that can be applied to virtually any CSM project. You will need to decide which are appropriate to your own organisation. They are listed in Figure 2.2.

First, you must identify customers' requirements – those things that are important to customers and will determine whether or not they are satisfied. Lots of things will be important to customers but some will be more important than others, so you must measure the relative importance of customers' requirements.

Second, you must measure satisfaction – how satisfied customers are with your organisation's performance on that same list of customer requirements. It is very useful, though not an essential part of measuring satisfaction, if you can go a step further and get a comparison with other organisations. This will give you a benchmark, because if you carry out a CSM study for your organisation in isolation, you may achieve an apparently satisfactory set of results and draw the conclusion that you are doing well. For example, a large proportion of your customers may have stated that they are 'satisfied'. But what if your main competitor is getting 'top-box' scores? One of the main principles underlying a reliable CSM study is that it should reflect as closely as possible the way that real customers make their satisfaction judgement, and they do not make that decision in isolation. When determining their satisfaction with your organisation, customers will compare you, consciously or subconsciously, with other organisations.

Once we mention the idea of comparisons, managers often want to compare their company with its direct competitors, but that may not be the most useful thing to do for CSM purposes. Consider for a moment how the customer's mind works in this situation. Most customers are not so-called 'promiscuous consumers', changing allegiance all the time from one supplier to another. For example, most people do not go to a different supermarket each week for their food shopping. Even if they live in a town that has three or four of the major supermarkets, most people just go to one of those, perhaps because they're delighted, highly loyal customers or possibly because they're habitual customers, finding it easier to keep to the same routine. The point is that when most customers are making that comparison judgement of their supermarket, they don't compare it with other supermarkets which they hardly ever visit and know little about. They judge the service they get in the supermarket against the service they receive from their bank, on an aeroplane or in a hotel. And that's what most customers do in respect of most suppliers – they compare them not with direct competitors but with other organisations that they deal with, so that is what you need to do in your CSM study. Of course, if yours is a very promiscuous market where most customers habitually use several or many suppliers, it will be appropriate to make direct comparisons with competitors. Satisfaction benchmarking will be explored in more detail in Chapter 11.

Having generated importance and satisfaction measures, you can use them to produce some survey outcomes, and the first of those is to identify the PFIs – the priorities for improvement. Since it is rarely effective to try to improve everything all at once, efforts and resources need to be focused if they are to be effective. If you are going to focus on resources it clearly makes sense to concentrate on those areas that are likely to bring the greatest gain in customer satisfaction. That is one reason why you need the two sets of measures. As we'll see in Chapter 10, the PFIs are identified by looking at the gaps between the importance and satisfaction scores.

Fifth, you will need an overall measure of customer satisfaction. We can call it a satisfaction index and it will be an indicator that you will use to monitor progress from one year to the next, which brings us to our sixth objective: it will need to be updateable. Most tracking research relies for its comparability from one year to the next on asking exactly the same questions and comparing the answers, but that will not be possible for CSM studies. To recall our definition (Figure 2.1), the questions on your questionnaire will need to change as customers' requirements change if it is to provide an accurate measure of customer satisfaction. So you will need a satisfaction index that will provide a reliable, trackable indicator even if you have to ask customers different questions in the years ahead, which you surely will. Towards the end of Chapter 10 we will explain how to produce that reliable overall measure.

Finally, it is very useful, though not essential, to make an internal comparison of the CSM survey results to identify so-called 'understanding gaps'. If employees have an inaccurate understanding of customers' requirements or their ability to satisfy customers, such a comparison might help to pinpoint any areas where the organisation is failing to satisfy customers. An internal survey can therefore be a very useful aid to management decision making and will be outlined in Chapter 12.

Project planning

To avoid unnecessary delays, any project needs a strict timetable. Three months is a typical time scale for a CSM project carried out by an agency, including exploratory research and a main survey. A project carried out in-house by people who also have other responsibilities will usually take much longer, probably twice as long. Figure 2.3 shows an example of a schedule for a typical CSM study carried out by an agency.

Project week number	
1	Project kick-off meeting
2–3	Recruit focus groups
4	Run focus groups
5	Analyse focus group results, produce interim report, questionnaire design for the main survey
6	Interim review meeting
7–8	Telephone survey
9	Analysis
10	Report writing, presentation preparation
11	Final presentation to management
12	Staff feedback workshops

Figure 2.3   Customer survey schedule

3 EXPLORATORY RESEARCH

An accurate measure

Much of the detail that is covered in this book is based on the assumption that you will want an accurate measure of customer satisfaction. That is a very different exercise from simply carrying out a customer survey where you ask customers some questions which yield some feedback and some ideas. Getting a measure which is accurate is much more difficult.

There are two factors which, more than any others, determine the accuracy of CSM results:

- Asking the right questions
- Asking the right customers.

The first is the purpose of the exploratory research and is covered in this chapter. The second refers to sampling, which is the subject of Chapter 4.

Many organisations assume that designing a questionnaire for a customer survey is easy. They might arrange a meeting attended by a few managers who, between them, suggest a list of appropriate topics for the questionnaire. There are two problems with this approach. First, the questionnaire almost always ends up far too long because managers tend to keep thinking of more topics on which customer feedback would be useful or interesting. The second, and more serious, problem is that the questionnaire invariably covers issues of importance to the company's managers rather than those of importance to customers. This is fine if the objective is simply to understand customers' perceptions of how the organisation is performing in the specified areas, but it will not provide a measure of customer satisfaction.

Think back to our original definition (Figure 2.1). The survey will provide you with a measure of satisfaction only if the questions on the questionnaire cover those things that customers were looking for in the first place – those things that make them satisfied or dissatisfied. Therefore, if you want an accurate measure of satisfaction you must start by asking the customers what their main requirements are. What are the things most important to them when they are customers of your organisation? Those are the topics that must be included on your questionnaire.

Survey design

The best starting point for a CSM survey is therefore to carry out exploratory research which allows the customers to set the agenda – to tell you what are the main things that make them satisfied or dissatisfied, so that you can get the survey design right. A survey is no different to a product. If it's not designed well it won't work, and it is the exploratory research that will ensure that the survey design is right – in other words that it asks the right questions of the right people.

Exploratory research is qualitative as opposed to quantitative. Qualitative research involves getting a great deal of information from a small number of customers. Plenty of information is needed because at this stage you want to understand your customers, (in the case of CSM what's important to them as customers), so that you can include the right questions on the questionnaire. From qualitative research you gather much information and gain a large amount of understanding, but since it involves only small numbers of customers it won't be statistically reliable.

Quantitative research involves obtaining a small amount of information from a large number of customers. In CSM this happens at the main survey stage and it will be statistically reliable. In short, the qualitative (exploratory) research establishes the list of customers' main requirements, enabling an accurate questionnaire to be designed. The quantitative research (main survey) establishes statistically reliable measures of customer satisfaction.

To conduct exploratory research for CSM you must talk to some customers. You can either talk to them one at a time, so-called 'depth interviews', or in groups typically known as focus groups. We will now examine each of the exploratory research techniques in turn, starting with depth interviews.

Depth interviews

Depth interviews are usually face to face and one to one. The duration of a depth interview can range from 30 to 90 minutes depending on the complexity of the customer–supplier relationship. Depth interviews are more commonly used in business-to-business markets, where the customers are other organisations, so we will describe the depth interview process mainly in that context.

The first question is how many to conduct. As a generalisation, a typical number of depth interviews that would be carried out in a business market is twelve. A very small customer base might need fewer. A large and complex customer base would need more, but twelve is the average. In consumer or domestic markets a larger number of depth interviews, perhaps thirty, would be normal, but focus groups would be more commonly used for exploratory research in that type of market.

ORGANISING DEPTH INTERVIEWS

Since exploratory research is not statistically valid, it is not necessary to use any complicated sampling techniques to select your small sample. You just use your best judgement to ensure that you have a good mix of different types of customers. If your customers are other organisations, that might involve:

- a mix of high-value and lower-value customers;
- customers from different business sectors;
- different geographical locations;
- a range of people from the DMU (decision-making unit).

This last point is important because, if your customers are other organisations, there will usually be several individuals who are affected in some way by your product or service and they will communicate, formally or informally, to determine whether that customer is satisfied or dissatisfied. Your exploratory research, and later your main survey, must reach the full spectrum of these individuals if it is going to be accurate. So, for example, if your main contacts are in purchasing, don't just go and see purchasing people; visit some people from production, from quality, from design and any other people who might be members of the DMU.

Having decided whom to visit, you will need to arrange an appointment. You should therefore contact all the customers that you would like to interview, gain their agreement to participate and fix a convenient time. You should then send a letter to all participants confirming the appointment and summarising the purpose of the interview. A typical letter of introduction for a depth interview is shown in Figure 3.1.

CONDUCTING DEPTH INTERVIEWS

Identifying the customer requirements
The interviewer's prime objective in a depth interview is to encourage the respondent to say as much as possible. It is therefore a good idea to start with any topic of conversation that might encourage the respondent to talk. There might be some cues in the room (for example, photos of football teams or a golf trophy), but in the absence of any visible prompts, a good starting point

Dear—————

It is our intention at XYZ Ltd to conduct a survey to measure the satisfaction of our customers. Before conducting a formal survey, we are asking a small number of our customers, including you, to participate in personal interviews of approximately 1 hour in duration to clarify what is most important to you in your relationship with XYZ and how well you feel that we meet your needs in those areas. The purpose of these preliminary interviews is to ensure that our survey concentrates on issues that are relevant and important to customers.

I believe that this process needs to be carried out in a professional manner and have therefore appointed The Leadership Factor Ltd, an agency which specialises in this work, to carry out the exercise on our behalf. The work will be conducted by Mr John Brierley, who will contact you in the next few days to arrange a convenient time to visit you to carry out the personal interview.

Your responses will be treated in total confidence by Mr Brierley and we will receive only an overall summary of the results of the interviews. Of course, if there are any particular points that you would like to draw to our attention you can ask for them to be recorded and your name associated with them if you wish.

I would like to thank you in advance for helping us with this important exercise. We will let you know the outcome and also how we plan to respond to the findings. I regard this as a very important step in our aim of continually improving the level of service we provide to our customers.

Yours sincerely

XXXXXX
Chief Executive

Figure 3.1 Introductory letter for depth interview participants

is to ask the respondent to explain his/her role in the organisation and bring that round to how he/she is involved with your company as a customer. All of this is just an ice-breaker, designed to establish rapport with the respondent before getting into the main part of the interview.

A depth interview is not a conventional interview where the interviewer asks a sequence of short questions and the interviewee gives short answers. The purpose of the depth interview is to come to understand customers, to clarify the things that are important to them, to draw out the things that make them satisfied or dissatisfied as customers. To achieve that aim it is essential to encourage the respondent to talk as much as possible.

That said, it would obviously not be productive to ask closed questions – questions that can be answered with one-word answers. It is better to ask open questions. But even open questions can be answered quite tersely, so it is most effective to think in terms of asking indirect rather than direct questions.

An example of a direct question would be:

> What are the things that are important to you as a customer when you're buying widgets?

Direct questions of this nature will tend to elicit short and rather general answers, such as:

> Well, quality's important, and on-time delivery, and of course price is important, and service.

To get the kind of information you need from CSM exploratory research, you need to approach the subject in a much less direct way. The same question asked in an indirect way might go something like this:

> I'd like you to imagine that you didn't have a supplier of widgets and you had to start with a blank piece of paper and find one. I wonder if you could talk me through what would happen in this organisation from the first suggestion that you might need a supplier of widgets right through to the time when a supplier has been appointed and evaluated. As you talk me through the process, perhaps you could also point out the different people in your organisation who might be involved at different times. What sort of things would each of those people be looking for from this new supplier and what roles would they each play in the decision-making process?

This is not a question that will be answered briefly. Indeed, in some organisations it will stimulate an explanation of a very complex process that may continue for several minutes. While the respondent is talking through this process, it is useful to make two sets of notes on separate pieces of paper. On the first jot down anything that seems to be important to somebody – a list of customer requirements. And on the second write a list of all the different people who seem to be getting involved – the composition of the DMU. When the respondent has finished the explanation you can show him/her the two lists and ask if there is anything that should be added to either.

Even though this discussion may already have taken quite some time, the respondent may not have thought of absolutely everything that is of some importance to his/her organisation as a widget customer, so you may need to prompt them. Before starting the depth interviews, you should therefore talk to people in your own organisation and ask them what things they think are important to customers and build up a list of assumed customer requirements. Anything on that list that the respondent has not mentioned should be used as a prompt. For example:

> What about round-the-clock service visits? Would that be of any importance to anyone in your organisation?

If the answer is yes, the item should be added to the list of customer requirements. Once you have done some depth interviews, you can use as prompts anything that other customers have told you is important.

Clarifying the relative importance

After some prompting you should have generated a comprehensive list of things that are important to the customer, and it might be a very long list. In a business market there might easily be fifty things on this list, but you cannot have as many as fifty attributes on the questionnaire for the main survey. Fifteen would be the normal number of questions, twenty at the most. So from this long list you need to be able to select the things that are most important to customers. One way is simply to ask them. You could go down the list and ask them to rate each item in importance. The trouble with this approach is that virtually *everything* is important to customers.

Imagine you were interviewing a respondent about rail travel and had developed a long list of things that were important to him/her as a rail passenger. One of the items on the list might be 'the quality of the hot drinks from the buffet car'. How important is that? The respondent will probably say something like:

> It's very important. I wouldn't want weak tea, and certainly not cold tea.

Another requirement on the list might be the punctual arrival of the train. How important is that? The respondent will probably say:

> It's very important. Nobody wants the train to be late, do they?

If you simply ask customers to rate the importance of each item in a list of requirements, *everything* will be important. But what if you ask them to compare the importance of the cup of tea and the punctual arrival of the train?

> Which is more important, the temperature of the cup of tea or the punctual arrival of the train?

This much more precise question will be far easier for people to answer. For most rail passengers, of course, the punctual arrival of the train will be far more important. Using this 'forced trade-off' approach provides a much more accurate indication of the relative importance of items in a list of requirements. There are proprietary techniques which are based on it, such as Conjoint Analysis, but the problem with many of these is that they rely on trading off everything against everything else, which is quite feasible for six or seven attributes but might get a little tedious if there are fifty! For CSM exploratory research it is therefore necessary to use a forced trade-off technique that will provide the required degree of accuracy but can be administered in what remains of a one-hour depth interview. This is the approach we would recommend. Start by asking the respondent to select his/her top priority by asking:

> If you could only choose one thing from that list, which would be the single most important one to you as a customer?

The respondent might reply:

> Punctual arrival of the train.

Then ask them to give it a score between 1 and 10, where 10 is extremely important and 1 is of no importance at all. They will almost invariably score it 10 since it is their top priority. (Note: A 10-point numerical rating scale is only one of several scales which could be used. A full assessment of rating scales is provided in Chapter 8.)

Having established a tangible benchmark, you can ask the respondent to score everything else on the list for its importance compared with his/her top priority of 'punctual arrival of the train'. Using this forced trade-off approach will provide a more accurate reflection of the relative importance of each item and will generate a far wider range of scores than simply going down the list without establishing the 'top-priority' benchmark.

Once the depth interviews are completed, it is a simple task to average the scores given for each requirement. Those achieving the highest average scores are the most important requirements of customers generally, and these are the items that should be included on the questionnaire for the main survey. In practice, you will often find that if you take all items scoring an average of eight or more, you will end up with about the right number of around fifteen to twenty customer requirements for the main survey questionnaire.

It can also be enlightening to use one or two 'projective techniques' in depth interviews, but we will explore these in the context of focus groups, where they are more commonly used.

Focus groups

For CSM exploratory research focus groups are similar to depth interviews, except that instead of talking to just one customer, a discussion is held with six to eight customers. It is normal to run four focus groups, although more would be held for a complex customer base requiring segmentation. Where there are segments of customers who may hold very different views, it is normal to segment the groups. So, for example, the views of younger people and older people towards health care or pensions are likely to differ considerably. In this situation it is not productive to mix them in the same focus group, but better to run separate groups for younger and older customers.

RECRUITING FOCUS GROUPS

Recruiting focus groups can be time-consuming and difficult. Participants have to spend 90 minutes taking part in the group, typically in the evening after they have done a day's work, and they will have to travel to the venue, so you are asking quite a lot of them. Therefore focus group participants would normally be invited personally, perhaps at the point of sale, through street interviews or door-to-door canvassing. Telephone recruitment is also used when necessary, but personal recruitment tends to result in greater respondent commitment.

It is important to provide written confirmation of all the details, such as time, location and anything respondents need to bring with them, to minimise the risk of confusion. A sample confirmation letter is shown in Figure 3.2.

Recruiting respondents – getting their agreement to take part – is only half of the process; ensuring that they actually attend the group is the other half, and sometimes the more difficult half. Therefore, as well as reminding people the day before, usually by telephone, it is also normal to offer them an incentive to give them an extra reason to turn out on that cold winter night, instead of settling down by the fire to watch TV.

Cash is the most common incentive, and rates can vary from £10 to over £50, depending on many factors. Higher rates are needed in London than in the provinces, and the more affluent the customer, the larger the incentive needs to be. Another critical factor is the strength of the relationship between the customer and the supplier. The weaker this relationship, the more difficult it can be to generate any interest in or commitment to the focus groups on the part of the respondents. We were once simultaneously

---

XYZ Ltd: Customer discussion group

Dear————

Thank you for agreeing to take part in the customer discussion group for XYZ Ltd. This is an opportunity to express your views on what is important to you about [description of the service] and you can be assured that your feedback will be taken very seriously.

Your discussion group will be held on [date] at [time] at [location]. A map is included to help you find the venue.

This is a genuine Market Research Project, carried out in accordance with the Market Research Society Code of Conduct, and your opinions, identity and telephone number will be kept in the strictest confidence.

The discussion will last approximately 90 minutes and you will received £xx provided by XYZ Ltd as a thank-you for sparing the time and giving your views.

If you are unable to attend we would very much appreciate it if you would let us know. Please ring me (or speak to a colleague of mine) on 01484 517575.

If you wear spectacles for either close or distant work, please bring them with you.

I feel sure you will enjoy the group.

Yours sincerely

Emma Dowse
The Leadership Factor

Figure 3.2   Confirmation letter for focus group participants

recruiting and running two sets of focus groups for two clients in financial services. One was in telephone banking and, even with very high incentives, recruitment was difficult and the attendance rate very poor. The customers had no relationship with and little commitment to the supplier. The second client was a traditional building society. Many customers had had mortgages or savings accounts over a long period, had personally visited their local branch and were loyal customers. Although the topics for discussion were virtually identical for both groups, the building society customers were far easier to recruit and the attendance rate was 100 per cent.

Incentives are also used in business markets, for example a sum of £50 for tradespeople or shopkeepers, £100 and upwards for doctors, pharmacists and other professionals. Another alternative here is to link your focus groups with hospitality. Invite them to a football match, for example, and run the focus group before the match.

Focus groups are run in a wide range of venues, including hotels, the supplier's own premises if suitable accommodation exists, people's homes or professional studios. The last-mentioned are fully equipped with all the technology needed to video the discussion, audio-record it and, if required, to view the proceedings live behind a one-way mirror. It is a good idea to consider what kind of venue will make the participants feel most comfortable. It needs to be somewhere they are familiar with and somewhere they see as convenient. The local pub's function room, for example, will often work better for attendance rates than the smart hotel a few miles down the road.

RUNNING FOCUS GROUPS

Focus groups are run by a facilitator (sometimes called a moderator) who will explain the purpose of the group, ask the questions, introduce any activities and generally manage the group. The facilitator clearly needs to be an excellent communicator and an extremely good listener. He/she must also be strong enough to keep order, insist that only one participant is speaking at a time, prevent any verbose people from dominating the group and adhere to a time schedule. Since it is virtually impossible for the facilitator to take notes while all this is going on, it is normal practice to audio-record groups, enabling the facilitator to listen to the tapes afterwards in order to produce a summary report of the proceedings. As well as needing a high level of expertise, the facilitator must also be objective, which is why it is always preferable to use a third-party facilitator for focus groups, especially for CSM.

The group will often start with a few refreshments, giving an opportunity for participants to chat informally to break the ice. Once the focus group starts officially, it is very important to involve everybody right at the beginning. Some people may not feel very confident in this type of situation, and the longer they go without saying anything, the less likely it becomes that they will ever say anything, so you need to involve everyone at the outset. It is best to start with a couple of easy questions and literally go round the group and let everyone answer, even if you don't really need to know the answers to those particular questions.

Once everyone has said something, a CSM focus group is effectively divided into two halves. The first half is just like a typical focus group and uses various techniques to encourage participants to talk about the subject – and for CSM focus groups there is just one over-riding subject: what do they require as customers; what things are most important to them? Various techniques (often called projective techniques) can be used, and some are described in the next section. All are designed to stimulate people to think hard about the issues, effectively by taking indirect questioning a stage further, prompting participants to think and talk about the issues without asking direct questions. By using these techniques you almost always get more out of the discussion.

PROJECTIVE TECHNIQUES

Theme boards
One projective technique is grandly known as thematic apperception, which simply means using themes or images to uncover people's perceptions. Examples of the technique in action include asking people to draw pictures or cut pictures out of magazines which symbolise or remind them of whatever area of customer activity is being researched. It is an exercise that works well and people enjoy doing it, but it is very time-consuming. Consequently what we would typically do in CSM focus groups, since we only have half the time available for projective techniques, is cut the pictures out for them, mount the pictures on boards, called theme boards, and use these as the stimulus material. There would usually be one board showing images which are positive or congruent with the brand concerned, and one showing negative or incongruent images relating to the product/service in question. The focus group facilitator can then ask a very simple question, such as:

> Do any of these pictures remind you of anything to do with . . .[whatever the customer activity is].

Creative comparisons
A creative comparison is a projective technique that can be used in almost any exploratory research situation – depth interviews as well as focus groups, business customers as well as consumers. It is basically an analogy, comparing an organisation or product which may have few distinctive features with something else that has far more recognisable characteristics. A real example will give a flavour of the technique. The interview was being carried out for a large multinational chemical company, and one of the things

they wanted to know was what customers thought of them overall, that is, their image, and how that compared with what customers thought of their main competitor. Considering the general lack of differentiation among this type of company, asking a direct question on image would not be very productive. Using a creative comparison, the following question was posed to senior managers in the large organisations that were customers of this particular chemical supplier.

> I'm going to ask you to do something now that you might think is a little bit unusual, but please bear with me and let's see how it goes. Let's imagine Company A was a famous sports personality; who would they be? And let's imagine Company B was also a famous sports personality; who would they be? Don't tell me straight away, have a think and then tell me.

The responses ranged from Frank Bruno to Mike Tyson, from Bobby Charlton to George Best and from Ian Botham to David Gower. Of course, the follow-up question is always:

> Can you explain why you chose xxxx for Company A and zzzz for Company B?

This elicits their deep feelings about those companies with respondents using phrases such as:

> They're a very big company but they're big and friendly. We have good personal relationships with them and we trust them.

> They're very aggressive, only interested in what's best for them, not what's best for the customer.

> They're very professional in everything they do.

> They're not as professional as they should be.

> They're very good – good products, good quality, good service, very good at what they do – but not altogether likeable. We don't get on very well with them and I don't think they always try very hard to look after us as a customer.

> An excellent company, very professional, excellent products but rather laid back, certainly no high-pressure selling involved. You sometimes wonder whether they even want the business.

The friendly Martian

The friendly Martian is one of the earliest projective techniques but it is particularly applicable to CSM exploratory research. In the depth interview section we suggested that a good approach is to ask respondents to talk through the decision process in order to get some clues about which things are important to them as customers. The friendly Martian technique is an even more indirect way of approaching this, and you can use it for virtually any CSM exploratory research, with all kinds of customers in focus groups or depth interviews. Imagine you were running CSM focus groups for a restaurant. In that context, the friendly Martian technique would be introduced as follows:

> Let's imagine that a friendly Martian (an ET-type character) comes down from outer space. He's never been to the earth before, and you have to explain to this friendly Martian how to arrange to have a meal out in a restaurant. What kind of things should he look out for, what does he need to know, what kind of things should he avoid? You've got to help this little guy to have a really good night out and make sure he doesn't end up making any mistakes. What advice would you give him?

Since the little Martian doesn't know anything, respondents will go into much more detail and mention all kinds of things that they would have taken for granted if you had asked a direct question.

GENERAL DISCUSSION

As well as projective techniques, general discussion can also be very effective in uncovering issues of importance to customers. Using the restaurant example again, relevant questions that will stimulate wide-ranging discussions in CSM focus groups include:

> What kind of things make you really enjoy a meal out? What kind of things make you feel like complaining when you have a meal out?

> What do you like most about Restaurant XXXX? What do you like least about Restaurant XXXX?

> Which different restaurants have you used? How do they compare with each other? What kind of things make some better than others?

Clarifying customers' main requirements

After some of the techniques outlined above have been used to compile a long list of things that are of some importance to customers, the remainder of the focus group needs to become much more structured. It should follow broadly the same steps that we outlined for the depth interview. First list on a flipchart all the customer requirements that have been mentioned in the discussions during the first half of the focus group. See if anybody can think of any more to add, then ask all participants to nominate their top priority as a benchmark and give it a score out of ten. This should be done on an individual basis, not collectively as a group. It is best to give out pencils and answer sheets, enabling everybody to write down their individual views.

When everybody's top priority has been established, each participant can read down the list and give every customer requirement a score out of ten, to denote its relative importance compared with their top priority. When this is completed, you can work out the average scores given by all the participants and, typically, all those averaging above eight, or the top fifteen, will be used in the questionnaire for the main survey.

4 SAMPLING

In principle sampling is simple. Most organisations have a large population of customers, but to get an accurate CSM result it is not necessary to survey all of them; you can use only a relatively small sample, provided that sample is representative of the larger population. However, there are several different types of sample, as summarised in Figure 4.1.

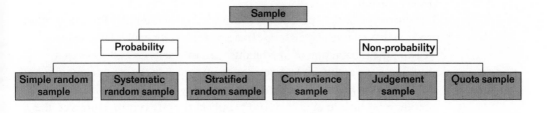

Figure 4.1   Sampling options

Probability and non-probability samples

The fundamental distinction between samples is whether they are probability or non-probability samples. A probability sample is often called a random sample and only this kind of sample can be relied upon to be without bias. The definition of a random sample is that everybody in the population should stand an equal chance of ending up in the sample. The most obvious example of a random sample is the UK National Lottery. Every ball remaining in 'Arthur' or 'Merlin' stands an equal chance of being the next ball to drop out. Non-probability samples tend to suffer from problems relating to bias, as shown in the next section.

NON-PROBABILITY SAMPLES

Convenience samples
The simplest form of non-probability sample is a convenience sample. Imagine you were conducting an opinion poll. You could go into the street

and ask the first fifty people you met how satisfied they were with the performance of the government. It would be quick, easy and cheap, but it would not be very representative. That might sound obvious, but it is easy for apparently sophisticated samples to degenerate into convenience samples, as we'll see later.

Judgement sample

The next form of non-probability sample, is a judgement or judgemental sample. That was precisely the kind of sample we suggested for the exploratory research, and whereas they are fine for qualitative research which does not purport to be statistically robust, they're not suitable for the main survey or any study which has to provide a statistically reliable result.

Quota sample

The third type of non-probability sample is a quota sample, and this is often used to survey large populations. Imagine that a city council wanted to measure the satisfaction of inhabitants with the facilities and services it provides. Let's assume it had decided to interview in the street a quota sample of 500 people who were resident within the city. It might appoint five interviewers, each to interview 100 people in the city centre. However, the interviewers would not be permitted to interview a convenience sample of the first 100 people who came along. A quota sample would require each interviewer to meet a number of carefully defined quotas in order to make their sample representative of the local population. The quotas would probably be based on the population statistics held by the city council which show how the population breaks down into groups. So, for example, they might show that 15 per cent of the population was aged 21 to 30, 18 per cent of the population was between 31 and 40 years old and so on. There may also be other segments such as gender, income levels, ethnic groups and residential neighbourhood. If the city council wanted its sample to be representative, all those groups would have to be represented in the same proportions in the sample as they appear in the total population. To achieve this the interviewers would be set quotas. In this example, 15 of the 100 people they each interview would have to be aged 21–30, 18 would have to be aged 31–40 and these would be overlaid with quotas for the other groupings such as gender, income and so on.

Let's assume that all five interviewers spent the entire working week, Monday to Friday, from 9 a.m. to 5 p.m. each day, interviewing in the city centre so that, by the end of the week, they had each completed 100 interviews and met all their quotas. That would yield a sample of 500 which would be totally representative of the population of the city, but it was not randomly selected and it would not therefore be without bias. The definition of a random sample stated that everybody in the population concerned must stand an equal chance of ending up in the sample. In this example, only those people in the city centre between 9 a.m. and 5 p.m. on weekdays would stand any chance of being sampled. So it would inevitably be biased, probably towards older people, the unemployed and people who worked in the city centre. In reality, of course, people try to minimise the problem of bias in quota samples by interviewing in a number of locations and at various times, but you can never eliminate it because it will remain the case that only those people in those locations at those times will stand any chance of being sampled, so, in theory, it can never be a random, and totally unbiased, sample.

PROBABILITY SAMPLES

Simple random sample
If you want to be sure of having an unbiased sample, it has to be random. As we said earlier, the National Lottery is the best-known example of a random sample, and that would be a simple random sample – each time another ball is required it is randomly sampled from all those remaining in the 'population'. However, that would be rather a long process if you needed a large sample from a large population, so in the days before sophisticated computer programs market researchers invented a less time-consuming way of drawing a simple random sample, strictly known as a 'systematic random sample'.

Systematic random sample
To produce a systematic random sample for a CSM survey you would first print your list of customers. Let's say there were 1000 customers on that list and you wanted a sample of 100, which is 1 in 10 of the population. You would first generate a random number between 1 and 10. Say it came out as 7. You would include in your sample the 7th name on the list, the 17th, the 27th and every 10th name thereafter, resulting in a systematic random sample of 100 customers. Before you generated that number, which was randomly generated, every customer on the list stood an equal chance of being included in the sample. So it would be a random sample, but it might not be representative, especially in a business market. It is not uncommon in business markets for some customers to be much more valuable than others. Sometimes, a very large proportion of a company's business, perhaps 40 or 50 per cent, might come from the top five or six customers. With a simple or systematic random sample, it would be quite possible that not one of those top five or six customers would end up in the sample. Clearly it would not make sense to undertake a survey to measure customer satisfaction which totally ignored 40-50 per cent of everything that business did. In a business market where most companies have a small number of high-value customers

and a larger number of low-value customers, a simple or systematic random sample will inevitably be dominated by the small customers. To achieve a sample which is representative as well as unbiased, stratified random sampling has to be used.

Stratified random sample

Producing a stratified random sample involves first dividing the customers into value segments or strata and then sampling randomly within each segment. We will work through an example of how this would be done in a typical business-to-business context. The first step in a business market is to take the database of customers and sort it in order of customer value, starting with the highest-value customer and going right through to the lowest-value. Then you would typically divide the list into three value segments – high-value, medium-value and low-value customers and then sample within each segment. The process is summarised in Figure 4.2.

Value segment	% of turnover	% of sample	No. of customers	Sampling fraction
High	40	40	40	2:1
Medium	40	40	160	1:2
Low	20	20	400	1:10

Figure 4.2   Stratified random sampling

In the example shown, the company derives 40 per cent of its turnover from its high-value customers. The fundamental principle of sampling in a business market is that if a value segment accounts for 40 per cent of turnover (or profit, or however you decide to define it), it should also make up 40 per cent of the sample. If the company has decided to survey a sample of 200 respondents, 40 per cent of the sample would mean that 80 respondents are required from the high-value customers. There are 40 high-value customers, so that would mean a sampling fraction of 2:1, meaning two respondents from each customer in the high-value segment. In business markets it is common practice to survey more than one respondent from the largest customers.

The medium-value customers also account for 40 per cent of turnover, so they must make up 40 per cent of the sample. That means the company needs 80 respondents from its medium-value customers. Since there are 160 customers in that value segment, the sampling fraction would be 1:2, meaning one respondent from every two medium-value customers. This would necessitate a random sample of one in every two medium-value customers. This could be easily produced using the same systematic random sampling procedure described earlier. First generate a random number between 1 and 2. Let's say it came out as 2. You would take the 2nd medium-value customer on the list, the 4th, the 6th and so on.

Finally, 20 per cent of the company's business comes from low-value customers, so they must make up 20 per cent of the sample, requiring 40 respondents in this example. There are 400 low-value customers, which would mean a sampling fraction of 1:10. This could be produced using the same systematic random sampling procedure. By the end of the process the company would have produced a stratified random sample which was randomly selected and so would be without bias and representative of its business.

SAMPLING STEPS

We will now review the steps you should go through to produce a sample. They are summarised in Figure 4.3.

---

1   Is random sampling feasible?
2   Define the 'sampling frame'
3   Determine the sample size
4   Identify segments or 'strata'

Figure 4.3   Sampling steps

1   Feasibility of random sampling

The first thing you have to ask is whether you can do a random sample at all. If you don't know who your customers are you cannot do a random sample because it is not possible to produce a list of the whole 'population' to sample from. Most retailers, for example, do not know who their customers are. They would not be able to print a list of the names of their population of customers. They are desperately trying to find out, of course, which is one reason why there are so many loyalty cards. Organisations in that situation would typically use a quota sample.

2   The sampling frame

If you know who your customers are, you can and should do a random sample, and the first step is to define your sample frame. This is the list of customers that you are going to sample from, and defining it is a policy decision. If you have diverse customer groups with very different customer requirements, you may need to do different surveys for different groups, and so you might want to start off by only measuring certain customer groups. Some organisations (for example financial services and utilities) usually need to distinguish between 'contact' and 'non-contact' customers because there can be a big difference between ordinary customers who just pay the monthly or annual premiums or the quarterly electricity bills ('non-contact' customers) and those who have had a much greater degree of contact, perhaps because they have made a claim or had some repair work carried out on their property ('contact' customers). There will be a lot of questions that are important to 'contact' customers that would not be appropriate for 'non-contact' customers, so in those circumstances it may be necessary to conduct two separate surveys.

Even organisations with a much more homogenous customer base still need to define their sampling frame. Typically organisations would measure customer satisfaction annually, and the sampling frame, the 'population', would be all customers who have dealt with the organisation in the last 12 months. However, that may not be appropriate for everyone. For example, it would not be very productive for an IT help desk measuring the satisfaction of its internal customers to question a customer about his or her experience of using the help desk 11 months previously. In such circumstances it would be more usual to use a much shorter time frame, perhaps all customers using the help desk in the last month. This may necessitate continuous tracking, where customers are surveyed every month and the results are rolled up for periodic reporting, perhaps quarterly, or even annually if there are not many customers.

So, as you can see, the definition of the 'customers' being surveyed may differ between different organisations, and that is a policy decision; but you must have a clear definition. It is those customers who will form the population for the survey, that is, the sampling frame.

3   Sample size

The next question to tackle is the number of customers you need in the sample. Some companies, typically in business-to-business markets, have a very small number of high-value accounts. Other companies have over a million customers. In a business market the size of the population is actually the number of individuals at each customer site who influence the satisfaction judgement of that customer – and that is not necessarily the same thing as the number of individuals with whom you have regular contact. Typically, the higher-value the customer, the more individuals will be involved. For computer software there may be several hundred users at one customer site. So the starting point is not how many customers are in the population, but how many individuals. Even so, some organisations will have much larger populations than others, but this will not affect the number of customers they need to survey for a reliable sample.

Statistically the accuracy of a sample is based on the absolute size of the sample, regardless of how many people are in the total population. Asking what proportion of customers should be surveyed is not relevant. A larger sample will always be more reliable than a smaller sample, whatever the size of the total population. This is best demonstrated by the normal distribution curve (see Figure 4.4) which basically tells us that whenever we examine a set of data it tends to follow this normal distribution. It does not apply only to research data. We might, for example, be looking at the average rainfall in Manchester in June over the last 300 years. We might see that in some years

Extreme data   **Normal data**   **Extreme data**

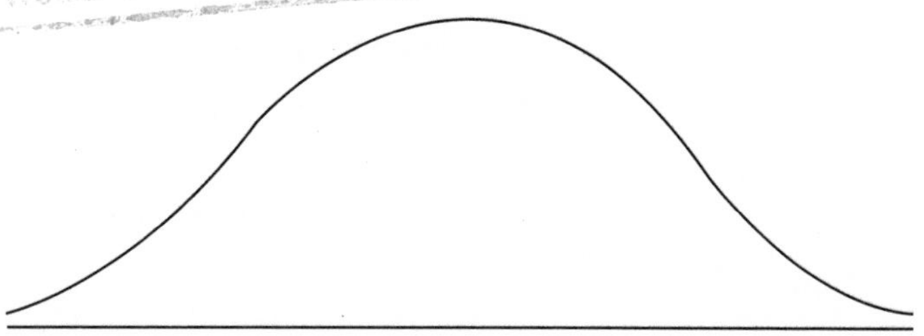

Figure 4.4 Normal distribution curve

there has been virtually no rainfall in June (even in Manchester), for a few years there has been an incredibly high rainfall, but for most years the rainfall in June falls somewhere between those extremes in the 'normal' zone. Whether we are looking at data from a research survey or about rain in Manchester, the key question is this:

What is the risk of abnormal data skewing the overall result?

The smaller the sample, the greater the risk.

For example, if you recorded the rainfall in June in Manchester over a five-year period when three of the years experienced normal June rainfall but two had exceptionally wet Junes, the average rainfall calculation would be heavily skewed by the two unseasonably wet months. If the data had been collected over 100 years, two exceptionally wet or dry months would make little impact on the overall result for the average June rainfall in Manchester. The principle is the same with surveys. If you survey only 10 people and two of them happen to hold extreme views, they would skew the overall result very heavily. They would make much less impact on a sample size of 50 and virtually no impact on a sample of 500, so the larger the sample, the lower the risk of getting a rogue result. Figure 4.5 shows that as the sample size increases, so does its reliability. At first, with very small sample sizes the reliability increases very steeply, but as the sample size grows there are diminishing returns in terms of reliability from any further increases in sample size. You can see that the curve starts to flatten in the 30 to 50 respondents zone, and this is typically said to be the threshold between qualitative and quantitative studies. By the time the sample size has reached 200, the gains in reliability from increasing the number of respondents in the sample are very small. Consequently, a sample size of 200 is widely considered to be the minimum sample size overall for adequate reliability in CSM. Companies with a very small population (around or below 200) should simply carry out a census survey.

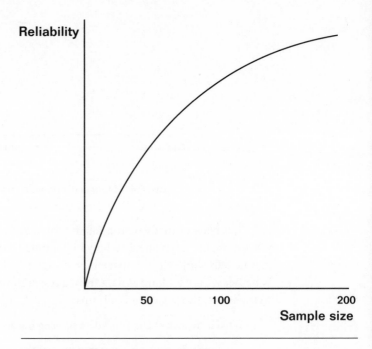

Figure 4.5   Sample size and reliability

There is one additional point to make here. The recommended sample size of 200 for adequate reliability means responses and not the number of customers sampled and invited to participate. Moreover, for statistical reliability, it means 200 customers sampled and the same 200 participating – completing the interview or returning the questionnaires. If the response rate is low, it is not reliable statistically to compensate by simply sending more questionnaires out until you have achieved 200 responses. The problem of 'non-response bias' can be a considerable one in CSM studies and will be explored in more detail in the next chapter.

4   Segments

As stated earlier, it is generally held in commercial research that a sample of 200 gives you adequate reliability for an overall measure of customer satisfaction whether you have a population of 500 or 500 000. However, there is one major exception, and that arises if you have various segments and you want to split the overall result into groups and look at the differences in the satisfaction levels of various segments. If you divide that sample of 200 into many segments, you will end up with the problem of small and therefore unreliable sample sizes for each segment. Therefore it is generally accepted that the minimum overall sample size is 200 and the minimum size per segment is 50.

As a consequence, your total sample size will often be determined by how many segments you want to divide the results into. If you want to break it down into six segments you would need a sample of at least 300 to get 50 in every segment. This can have a significant implications for companies with multiple branches or outlets. On the basis of 50 per segment, a retailer with 100 stores would need a sample of 5000 if customer satisfaction is to be measured at store level. However, our view is that if comparisons are to be made between stores, and management decisions taken on the basis of the results, an absolute minimum of 100 customers per store should be surveyed and preferably 200. For a retailer with 100 stores, this would result in a total sample size of 10 000 or even 20 000 customers for a very reliable result at store level.

Sampling summary

Figure 4.6 summarises the three main elements of producing a reliable sample. First, to be reliable a sample must be representative of your business, and in a business market that will mean in terms of customer value. In a consumer market there may be other segments, typically demographic ones, that you may see as more relevant.

1   Representative
   • By customer value
   • By segment

2   Random – without bias
   • Companies
   • Individuals

3   Adequate size
   • 200 minimum
   • 50 per segment

Figure 4.6   Sampling summary

Second, the sample must be randomly selected if it is to be without bias. Since surveys are not completed by companies but by individuals, if you operate in a business-to-business market you will have to decide which individuals. Very often the individuals are chosen on the basis of convenience – the people most commonly dealt with whose names are readily to hand. If the individuals are selected on this basis it will mean that however carefully a stratified random sample of companies has been produced, at the eleventh hour it has degenerated into a convenience sample of individuals whom somebody knows. To avoid that intrusion of bias you should randomly sample the individuals. This can be done by compiling a list of individuals who are affected by your product or service for each customer in the sample and then selecting the individuals randomly from that list. If you want to add complication, but also accuracy, you should stratify the list of individuals to avoid getting too many peripheral ones. For example, you might analyse the DMU and decide that to reflect the decision-making process accurately, your sample should be made up of 40 per cent purchasing contacts, 40 per cent technical contacts and 20 per cent from all other types of contact. If so, you should randomly sample the individuals in those proportions.

Finally, we said that a sample must be large enough. And that means at least 200 in your total sample and an absolute minimum of 50 in each sub-group that you want to analyse separately.

5 SURVEY OPTIONS

Having completed the exploratory research and the sampling, you are now ready to carry out the main survey. The first step here is to decide what kind of survey, in other words, how the data will be collected. There are three basic options:

- Personal interviews
- Telephone interviews
- Self-completion questionnaires.

In this chapter we will examine the options, looking at the advantages and disadvantages of each one, in order to help you decide which is most suitable for your organisation.

PERSONAL INTERVIEWS

Advantages
In an ideal world personal interviews would be used for most surveys because they have a number of important advantages:

- It is easier to build rapport with the respondent in the face-to-face situation.
- It is much easier to achieve total respondent understanding. Not only can things be explained, but with face-to-face interviews it is also usually possible to see if the respondent is having a problem with the question.
- Visual prompts such as show cards can be used to show respondents the range of responses on a rating scale, for example.
- Complex questions become more feasible because they can be more easily explained.
- Personal interviews can be very cost-effective with a captive audience, such as passengers on a train, spectators at a football ground or shoppers in a busy store, because where there are plenty of people in one place it is often possible to conduct large numbers of interviews in a short time.
- It is usually possible to gather a good deal of qualitative information in addition to the straight scores because the interviewer can establish rapport with the respondents, who become more talkative as a result.
- In some situations, such as visiting people at home or at their place of work,

it is feasible to conduct quite long interviews, up to half an hour, allowing plenty of time to explore issues in some depth. Of course, some personal interviews, such as those on a windy street corner in January, will have to be much shorter.

Disadvantages

There are disadvantages to personal interviews, mainly relating to cost.

- Personal interviews will almost always be the most costly data collection option, especially in business-to-business markets, for two main reasons:

  (a) You need interviewers who can hold a proper conversation at the same level as the people they are interviewing. For customer satisfaction surveys in business markets the respondents will usually be senior people who will soon become irritated and often alienated from the process if they feel that the interviewer does not fully understand the topics under discussion.
  (b) Business customers are usually scattered over a wide geographical area, so more time may be spent travelling than interviewing. It is not unusual in business-to-business markets to average no more than two personal interviews per day. As well as the time involved, the travel itself is likely to be costly.

- Since many people do not like to give offence, there may be a tendency to be less frank in the face-to-face situation (giving low satisfaction scores, for example), especially if the interviewer is employed by or associated with the organisation conducting the survey.

TELEPHONE INTERVIEWS

Advantages

- Telephone interviews are the quickest way of gathering survey data.
- They are relatively low-cost and certainly much less costly than personal interviews.
- The two-way communication means that the interviewer can still explain things and minimise the risk of misunderstanding.
- It is possible to gather reasonable amounts of qualitative information in order to understand the reasons underlying the scores. For example, interviewers can be given an instruction to probe any satisfaction scores below a certain level to ensure that the survey identifies why customers are dissatisfied, not just that they are dissatisfied.
- Distance is not a problem, even in worldwide markets.

Disadvantages

- Interviews have to be short. Ten minutes is enough for a telephone interview, especially when interviewing consumers at home in the evenings. Up to 15 minutes is acceptable for business interviews during the day.
- Questions have to be quite short and straightforward. As we will see when we look at rating scales in Chapter 8, there are certain types of question that cannot be used on the telephone.
- One of the biggest frustrations with telephone surveys is that people do not seem to be sitting at the other end of the telephone line waiting to be interviewed! You must be prepared to make multiple callbacks to get a reliable sample, as shown by the statistics in Figure 5.1. In household markets the hit rate tends to be better than the figures shown in the table, but in business markets it can easily be worse. For that reason it would be good practice to make up to five callbacks for domestic interviews and up to eight in business markets to ensure good sampling reliability.
- Telephone surveys require good interviewers. For all interviews they need to be sufficiently authoritative to persuade respondents to participate in the interview and sufficiently relaxed and friendly to build rapport. As with personal interviews, telephone interviews in business markets need interviewers of high calibre who can communicate at the same level as the respondent.

Average number of attempts required to make contact in telephone surveys

1	attempt reaches	24% of the sample
5	attempts reach	75% of the sample
8	attempts reach	89% of the sample
17	attempts reach	100% of the sample

Figure 5.1 Multiple callbacks for accurate sampling

SELF-COMPLETION QUESTIONNAIRES

Self-completion questionnaires are usually administered in the form of a postal survey, although other methods of distribution such as fax, e-mail or point-of-sale questionnaires can be used. Whatever the distribution method, self-completion questionnaires are filled in alone by respondents without help from a researcher. They have a number of advantages.

Advantages

- Self-completion questionnaires will usually be the cheapest method of data collection for most surveys. However, there are many hidden costs such as handling and printing, which boost the real cost of postal surveys. The difference in cost between postal and telephone surveys is usually less than most people imagine.
- There is clearly no risk of interviewer bias.

- Most respondents will see a self-completion questionnaire as the least intrusive and most anonymous way of being surveyed.
- Self-completion questionnaires are ideally suited to surveys of internal customers. The postal cost can usually be avoided and, where e-mail is feasible, much of the printing and handling costs as well. Most important, it is easier to implement policies to ensure a good response rate, such as senior management endorsement, and for paper questionnaires you can hand them out and collect them at a predetermined time.
- For similar reasons, self-completion questionnaires are also good at the point of sale immediately after the 'customer experience'. It's a very low-cost way of collecting data, but it must not be voluntary (as in most hotels, for example), otherwise it will be a convenience sample. Voluntary point-of-sale surveys will almost certainly generate very low response rates and will consequently provide meaningless data as far as CSM is concerned (though they may be useful for other reasons, such as an additional complaints channel). Therefore, if you are going to survey customers at the point of sale, the questionnaires must be handed out, either to every customer or to a random sample, and collected to ensure a reliable response rate. However, you also need to be aware that this type of survey will be very heavily influenced by the customer's recent experience. A disappointing breakfast a few minutes earlier may result in poor satisfaction ratings across the board. So this type of 'post-transaction' survey may not give an accurate measure of customers' underlying satisfaction or a reliable guide to future purchasing behaviour. The irate customer who was made to wait too long to check out of the hotel may vow, in the heat of the moment, not to return, but some weeks later when next booking a hotel, the incident will have waned in importance and a more measured purchase decision will be made. For this reason, a periodic 'baseline' survey of customers away from the point of sale and the time of purchase will usually provide a much more accurate measure of underlying customer satisfaction.

Disadvantages

- Postal surveys are very slow. They also tend to suffer from low response rates. The generally accepted figure for an 'average' response rate for customer satisfaction surveys by post is 25 per cent, but this masks an extremely wide variation from below 10 per cent to over 90 per cent. Typically, the more important the topic is to the customer, the higher will be the base response rate. For example, a satisfaction survey of new car buyers is likely to generate a higher response rate than a survey by a utility company. In business markets customers are more likely to complete a survey for a major supplier than a peripheral one. Overall, the average response rate is 25 per cent although it is typically somewhat higher with business customers and lower with householders.

- Questionnaires must be short.
- Questions must be simple. People will tend to make a quick judgement about how time-consuming the questionnaire is going to be to fill in, and that will be a combination of the questionnaire's length and its perceived difficulty. Moreover, since questions cannot be explained to respondents, they must be very straightforward.
- One of the biggest disadvantages of most forms of self-completion survey is that as soon as you send it out you immediately abdicate control: you lose control over who fills it in and how it is filled in. You may have a painstakingly constructed sample of key decision-makers who receive the questionnaire and immediately pass it to a subordinate to complete. You also have no control or knowledge of how they fill it in – whether they rush it and give it very little thought, and even whether they understand the questions or the instructions. If there are any grounds for suspicion that a questionnaire has been incorrectly completed, it should be discarded as invalid.
- By far the main disadvantage of self-completion questionnaires, however, is the problem of unrepresentative samples. If a self-completion questionnaire achieves an 'average' response rate of 25 per cent, is it possible to say that the views expressed by the 25 per cent who returned the questionnaire are the same as the views held by the 75 per cent who did not? In fact, it has been demonstrated by tests that self-completion surveys with low response rates suffer from the problem of 'non-response bias'. Some forms of bias, such as demographic bias, can be corrected. For example, a survey of householders is more likely to be returned by retired people than by busy parents who both have careers. This type of age-related bias could be corrected at the analysis stage, but it is not possible to correct attitude bias. Tests demonstrate that non-response bias is often an attitude problem, with customers at the extremes of the normal distribution curve over-represented. In other words, the questionnaire is completed by the most satisfied customers as an act of loyalty and by anybody who sees it as a convenient medium for grumbling, moaning and complaining. The problem is that you just do not know what the other 75 per cent think, and without surveying them there is no way of finding out!
- The lower the response rate, the bigger the problem of non-response bias. It is a general rule of thumb in the research industry that a response rate of at least 50 per cent is required to reduce the problem to acceptable proportions. In theory, of course, any response rate below 100 per cent will have an element of non-response bias, so a target of 65 per cent rather than 50 per cent for a reliable result seems more reasonable.

Many people work on the mistaken principle that to increase the reliability of postal surveys with disappointing response rates they simply need to send more questionnaires out in order to get more back. This is totally mistaken. The problem is not the size of the response but the response rate. Only by improving the response rate can you overcome the problem of non-response bias.

If you want an accurate measure of customer satisfaction, non-response bias is clearly a fundamental problem. It suggests a serious doubt about the acceptability of the postal method of data collection. If you need a 65 per cent response rate for adequate reliability, you either have to work very hard to maximise the response rate or opt for a method of data collection such as telephone where that level of response will be more easily achievable.

6 MAXIMISING RESPONSE RATES

Probably the most common question that we are asked when presenting our seminar on Customer Satisfaction Measurement is how to improve response rates on postal surveys. For anybody aiming to use this approach to measure customer satisfaction it is a vital question since the problem of non-response bias can invalidate the whole exercise if the response rate is low. Moreover, you should not forget the point of the exercise. Measuring customer satisfaction is not just a matter of carrying out a customer survey, asking a few questions and getting some feedback. It is meant to be a measure, usually one that is monitored over time as a key indicator of organisational performance, so an inaccurate measure is worse than no measure at all.

To provide an accurate measure of customer satisfaction a response rate below 50 per cent cannot be relied on. You need to get over 50 per cent and preferably over 65 per cent, which is a very tall order in some markets. However, due to the high level of interest in response rates, quite a large body of knowledge now exists on the subject. This chapter reviews the experiments, the academic literature and the experience of practitioners to provide a comprehensive guide to maximising response rates.

Techniques to boost response rates can be divided into four categories:

- Essentials
- Advisables
- Marginals
- Avoidables.

Essentials

Some things are essential to achieving an adequate response rate. They include:

- Accurate database
- Reply-paid envelope
- Follow-up strategy
- Introductory letter.

ACCURATE DATABASE

Of top priority, especially in business markets, is an accurate, up-to-date database including contact names and correct job titles. The accuracy of business databases can erode by 30 per cent per annum, so you may easily be mailing lots of incorrectly addressed questionnaires.

REPLY-PAID ENVELOPE

A postage-paid reply envelope is now expected by respondents and all research studies show a significantly reduced response rate if it is omitted. Some people are tempted to try fax-back questionnaires in business markets on the grounds that it might be easier for respondents to simply pop it in the fax machine. Tests show this assumption to be mistaken. Many people in large offices do not have easy access to a fax machine. Therefore, by all means include a fax-back option and a prominent return fax number, but include a reply-paid envelope as well.

FOLLOW-UP STRATEGY

A follow-up strategy is also widely endorsed by the research studies. The word 'strategy' is important because more than one reminder will continue to generate additional responses, albeit with diminishing returns. A multiple follow-up strategy has been widely reported to have a positive effect on response rates. The more intensive the follow-up strategy, the better the results. The ultimate follow-up strategy involves a four-step approach, as shown in Figure 6.1.

Step 1	Post card to everyone in the sample after one week. This doubles as a thank-you for respondents and a reminder for non-respondents.
Step 2	After a further 10 days, reminder letter and duplicate questionnaire to all non-respondents.
Step 3	Telephone follow-up of non-respondents after a further 10 days.
Step 4	Final written follow-up of non-respondents with another duplicate questionnaire after a further 10 days. This final mailed reminder to be sent recorded delivery.

Figure 6.1   Multiple follow-up strategy

This intensive follow-up strategy can more than double response rates, with as much as 83 per cent being achieved in experiments. The obvious disadvantages are the time and cost involved, although as the cost of the follow-up steps increases there should be fewer non-respondents left to chase. Second, the system relies on the ability to identify respondents, so unless the replies are sent to a neutral third party it will have a negative effect on the perceived confidentiality of the exercise.

INTRODUCTORY LETTER

The introductory letter accompanying the questionnaire is likely to be more effective than any single step of the follow-up strategy. It should concentrate on explaining why it is in the respondent's own interest to complete the questionnaire. This is supported by several studies showing significantly higher response rates when respondents are interested in the aims and outcomes of the research, compared with less specific surveys aimed at the general public. Appeals (to public duty, to good causes and so on) have been shown by academic research to be ineffective. Academic tests have shown that covering letters offering feedback on the results have a significant positive impact on response rates. Practitioner experience supports this, especially in business markets. In our view a good covering letter, highlighting benefits to respondents and promising feedback, will boost response rates by around 30 per cent on average. Both the introductory letter and post-survey feedback to customers will be covered in more detail later in this book.

Advisables

Three more measures which are generally agreed to boost response rates, although by a lower margin, are:

- Pre-notification
- Questionnaire design
- Money.

PRE-NOTIFICATION

The effectiveness of pre-notification has been shown by several academic studies. Their conclusion is that this measure almost always works, with telephone pre-notification the most costly but most effective method (doubling response rates in some studies). Mail pre-notification has a small but positive effect in consumer markets, but the research is inconclusive for business markets, although our own experience demonstrates a strong effect when pre-notification letters are sent to business customers for telephone surveys. For postal surveys in business markets we advise sending the introductory letter with the questionnaire, supported where feasible by personal pre-notification from sales people. A recent innovation, suitable only for large companies with many customers and big budgets, has been the use of mass communications media such as TV advertising to notify people of a forthcoming survey and its benefits to customers.

QUESTIONNAIRE DESIGN

Questionnaire design, rather than length, is a significant factor. If respondents' initial impression is that the questionnaire will be difficult to complete, the response rate will be depressed. Academic research shows that apart from very long questionnaires, length is a less significant factor, so it is better to have clear instructions and a spacious layout spreading to four sides of A4, rather than a cluttered two-page questionnaire. More specifically, research suggests that it makes no difference to response rates whether people are asked to tick boxes or circle numbers/words, nor whether space is included for additional comments.

MONEY

Money also seems to be a motivator! Not incentives generally, but money specifically. And money *now*! Research in the USA has shown that a quite modest monetary reward, such as $1 attached to the introductory letter, will have a significant effect in business as well as domestic markets. However, it is important that the money goes with the questionnaire. Future promises of payment to respondents are less effective and 'birds in the bush', such as prize draws, much less effective. Some people rather scurrilously suggest that researchers can reduce costs by enclosing money only with the first reminder, a tactic you might get away with if you have a sample of individuals who are unlikely to communicate with each other!

Marginals

The evidence for some response-boosting techniques is much more equivocal. These include:

- Use of colour
- Postage rate
- Anonymity.

USE OF COLOUR

The use of colour is a contentious issue. Some people advocate the use of coloured envelopes or the printing of relevant messages on envelopes. However, it is generally accepted that 10 per cent of mailshots are filed unopened in the bin, so if your envelope suggests junk mail you are likely to depress response by 10 per cent. Sticky address labels are also associated with mailshots, so we advise using plain white window envelopes.

Use of colour on the questionnaires should also be considered. It is generally accepted that the use of more than one colour for printing the questionnaire will enhance clarity of layout and ease of completion and will therefore boost response rates. Printing the questionnaire on coloured paper may also help, presumably because it is more conspicuous to people who put it on one side, intending to complete it in a spare moment. The NatWest Bank reported a 13 per cent improvement in response rates as a result of an experiment with questionnaires printed on pink paper. A 1977 academic test even found the colour of signatures on covering letters to be a significant variable. It recommended green signatures as best, with blue being the least effective! However, a very large split test by Cranfield University and the Manchester Business School in 1997 demonstrated that there is nothing to be gained from using coloured paper on questionnaires. In fact, in their test, the questionnaires on white paper achieved slightly higher response rates.

POSTAGE RATE

There is some evidence from academic research that the use of first-class mail for mail-out and reply envelopes will help response rates slightly. The type of stamp used is also an issue. The use of a real stamp rather than a franking machine or a mailsort stamp will help response rates, as the latter are associated with mailshots.

ANONYMITY

It is conventional wisdom that response rates and accuracy will be higher where respondents are confident of anonymity and confidentiality. Practitioner evidence strongly supports this view for employee satisfaction surveys and most types of satisfaction surveys in business markets, where the respondent envisages an ongoing personal relationship with the supplier. In mass markets, where personal relationships are normally absent, there is no conclusive evidence that anonymity increases response, although in potentially sensitive areas such as financial services anonymity is preferable. Of course, there is a trade-off here with follow-up strategies, which will be much more cost-effective if respondents are required to identify themselves. In many consumer markets it may therefore be better to ask respondents to identify themselves in order to improve the cost-effectiveness of follow-up strategies.

Avoidables

There are some frequently used response-boosting techniques that are eminently avoidable since there is no conclusive evidence that they consistently improve response rates. Indeed, they may reduce quality of response and they are usually costly. Mainly concerning various types of incentive, avoidables include:

- Incentives
  - Prize draws
  - Free gift
  - Coupons
  - Donations to charity
- New media.

INCENTIVES

Research carried out in the USA suggests that the chance of future monetary reward, such as a prize draw, makes no difference unless it is very large. Also in the USA, academic tests report no effect from the promise of a donation to charity. Recent research in the UK suggests that the inclusion of discount coupons can even depress response rates, perhaps because they give the impression that the survey is sales-driven. Even increasing the value of coupons has no effect, suggesting that redeemable discount coupons are not seen as being monetary in nature. Perhaps more surprisingly, tests also show that the inclusion of a free gift (other than money) does not boost and may reduce response rates, presumably because of its association with mass mailings.

NEW MEDIA

At the time of writing, postal surveys get a much better response rate than new media such as IVR (interactive voice response), which involve a computerised telephone interview with synthesised voice and require the respondent to use keys on their telephone to answer questions.

Summary

Introductory letter	30%
First reminder letter	25%
Telephone reminder	25%
Respondent-friendly questionnaire	20%
Advance-notice letter	15%
Incentive	< 15%
Second reminder letter	12%
Envelope	+/– 10%

Figure 6.2 Techniques for maximising response rates

Based on academic research, plus the experience of ourselves and other practitioners, Figure 6.2 indicates the average effect on response rates of the measures reviewed in this chapter. The chart assumes a reasonable questionnaire, personally addressed, mailed to the correct address and including a postage-paid reply envelope. It suggests the likely increase in your base response rate. For example, a 20 per cent improvement on a 30 per cent response rate would result in a 36 per cent response rate. For customer satisfaction surveys base response rates are likely to be below 20 per cent in mass markets and around 30 per cent in closer relationship business markets. The following points should be borne in mind:

- The most effective way of increasing response is the inclusion of a good introductory letter which spells out why it is in the customer's interest to return the questionnaire. On average this will improve the base response rate by 30 per cent.
- Sending a postal reminder will improve response by a further 25 per cent. This should be done ten days after the original mailing, and a further copy of the questionnaire should be included in the letter.
- After another ten days a telephone reminder should yield a further 25 per cent improvement.
- A user-friendly questionnaire, not too long, attractively designed and with a couple of easy questions at the beginning, can add another 20 per cent.
- A further 15 per cent can be achieved by an advance-notice letter, sent a few days before the survey, which conditions respondents to expect the questionnaire.
- Many people mistakenly assume that an incentive is the best way to improve response rates. A large number of tests show that this is not the case. Most incentives have little or no effect and some tests have even shown a detrimental effect, typically by incentives such as prize draws or coupons which may be confused in respondents' minds with a selling approach. Even promises of charitable donations usually achieve little. It is therefore sensible to focus more attention on the alternative ways of increasing response which, in the main, are less costly and more effective.

- Even a second reminder letter can achieve a further 12 per cent which is more than most incentives.
- Some people claim that the envelope is a valuable communications medium which presents an opportunity to alert customers that a customer survey is enclosed, thus improving response. On the other hand, heavily overprinted envelopes are usually associated with mailshots and a selling approach. Evidence shows that 10 per cent of mailshots are filed in the bin unopened. To avoid this risk it is therefore preferable to send postal questionnaires in plain, personally addressed envelopes which will almost always be opened.

7 QUESTIONNAIRE DESIGN

The next activity, and one of the most critical, before the survey can be conducted is designing the questionnaire. The three broad aspects of questionnaire design that should be considered are the questions, the layout and rating scales. This chapter will cover the questions, including how they are worded plus the layout of the questionnaire, and Chapter 8 will examine the crucial issue of which rating scale to use.

The questions

Figure 7.1 shows a checklist. You could compare your questionnaire with this checklist and ask whether it breaks any of the rules.

---

1   Does the respondent have the knowledge?
❑ Many respondents feel they ought to have an opinion
❑ Qualify respondents before including them in the survey

2   Will the respondent understand the question?
❑ Ambiguity of common words
❑ Unfamiliar or jargon words
❑ Double question

3   Will the questions bias the response?
❑ Balanced question
❑ Balanced rating scale

Figure 7.1   Questionnaire checklist

1   RESPONDENT KNOWLEDGE

The first item to consider is whether respondents will possess the knowledge to answer the questions you have asked. Not having it won't stop them! People tend to think that they ought to have an opinion on things. You might be asking passengers at an airport for their views on the differences between economy- and business-class flights. Many people would answer those questions even if they have never flown business class. That would not be a problem if you want to understand economy-class passengers' perceptions of business-class travel, but it would be very misleading if you were trying to understand the real experiences of business-class customers. So, if you only wanted people who had flown business class, you would have to qualify respondents before including them in the survey.

2   UNDERSTANDING THE QUESTIONS

The second item to consider is whether the respondents will understand the questions, or, more accurately, whether they will all assign to the questions the same meaning as the author of the questionnaire. There are several potential problems here, often because many of the words we use quite happily in everyday speech are dangerous when used in questionnaires: they are simply not precise enough. A pertinent example is shown in Figure 7.2.

Which of the following newspapers do you read regularly?

Please tick the box next to any newspapers that you read regularly.

Express	❏	Mirror	❏
Guardian	❏	Sun	❏
Mail	❏	Times	❏

Figure 7.2   Ambiguous question

What exactly does the word 'regularly' mean? When the results of that question have been analysed, what will they tell anybody? 'Regularly' could mean anything from every day to once every four years on 29 February. When wording questions you must be extremely precise, to the point of being pedantic. You cannot afford any ambiguity or you may find that you have generated a meaningless set of results when your survey is complete. So the question about the newspapers would have to be phrased as in Figure 7.3.

Another reason why respondents misunderstand questions stems from the use of unfamiliar words. Everybody knows that it is not advisable to use jargon, but most people still underestimate the extent to which words they use all the time at work with colleagues can be jargon to customers. Of course, that is another very good reason for carrying out the exploratory research:

you can use the customer's terminology on the questionnaire rather than your own. As well as obviously technical names, even words such as facility and amenity are liable to ambiguity and misinterpretation.

How often do you read each of the following newspapers?

Please tick one box for each newspaper.

	Every day	More than once a week	Weekly	Monthly	Every 3 months	Less than once every 3 months	Never
Express	❑	❑	❑	❑	❑	❑	❑
Guardian	❑	❑	❑	❑	❑	❑	❑
Mail	❑	❑	❑	❑	❑	❑	❑
Mirror	❑	❑	❑	❑	❑	❑	❑
Sun	❑	❑	❑	❑	❑	❑	❑
Times	❑	❑	❑	❑	❑	❑	❑

Figure 7.3　Precise question

Double questions are a very common cause of misunderstanding and ambiguous survey results. A common example from customer surveys would be:

> Were the staff friendly and helpful?

Which characteristic do you want to know about? Friendliness and helpfulness are not the same, are they? If that question is scored poorly, indicating customer dissatisfaction, how would the organisation know what to change to put matters right? If you want to include both aspects of staff behaviour in the questionnaire, you must ask two questions.

3　INTRODUCING BIAS

Probably the biggest problem relating to the wording of questionnaires is the danger that the questionnaire itself will bias the response. There are two reasons why this might happen. First, the question itself and second, the rating scale. Typical questions on a customer satisfaction survey might be:

How satisfied are you with the variety of food on the menu?

How satisfied are you with the speed of response for on-site technical support?

How satisfied are you with the reliability of the product?

Each one of these questions has introduced an element of bias which is likely to skew the results, and the problem arises in the first part of the question:

How satisfied are you with . . . ?

The question itself suggests that customers are satisfied. It is just a matter of *how satisfied*. To eliminate that bias and be certain that the survey is providing an accurate measure of customer satisfaction, these questions should be worded as follows:

How satisfied or dissatisfied are you with the variety of food on the menu?

How satisfied or dissatisfied are you with the speed of response for on-site technical support?

How satisfied or dissatisfied are you with the reliability of the product?

The other element that might bias the response is the rating scale. Biased rating scales are commonly found on many customer satisfaction questionnaires, as shown in Figure 7.4.

Please comment on our quality of service by ticking one box on each line.

	Excellent	Good	Average	Poor
Helpfulness of staff	❑	❑	❑	❑
Friendliness of staff	❑	❑	❑	❑
Cleanliness of the restaurant	❑	❑	❑	❑
Cleanliness of the toilets	❑	❑	❑	❑
Waiting time for your table	❑	❑	❑	❑
Waiting time for your meal	❑	❑	❑	❑

Figure 7.4   A positively biased rating scale

The scale shown in Figure 7.4 is not balanced, and is likely to bias the result towards satisfaction. Most positively biased rating scales on customer satisfaction questionnaires are probably there because the questionnaire designers are oblivious of the problem. However, some companies which are very experienced in CSM deliberately use positively biased questionnaires on the grounds that only 'top-box' satisfaction matters, so it is only degrees of satisfaction that are worth measuring. We feel that there are two problems with this philosophy. First, even if most customers are somewhere in the very satisfied zone, it is still essential to understand just how dissatisfied the least satisfied customers are and the extent to which individual attributes are causing the problem. In many ways it is more valuable to the organisation to identify in detail the problem areas that it can fix than to have detailed information on how satisfied its most satisfied customers are. The second argument against using positively biased rating scales is that it is simply not necessary. If you have a sufficient number of points on the scale you can accommodate degrees of satisfaction and dissatisfaction in equal proportions, as shown in Figure 7.5.

Figure 7.5 is a balanced rating scale because it has an equal number of points above and below the mid point and, very important, the words at opposing points on the scale are exact opposites of each other. Whether or not it has a mid-point makes no difference to whether or not it is balanced. There is much interest in whether scales should have a mid-point. Strictly speaking, a scale should have a mid-point on the grounds that it is not valid research to force anyone to express an opinion they don't hold. For example, an interviewer may approach people in the street and ask them:

How satisfied or dissatisfied are you with the reliability of our delivery times?

Tick one box.

Totally satisfied ☐

Very satisfied ☐

Quite satisfied ☐

Neither satisfied nor dissatisfied ☐

Quite dissatisfied ☐

Very dissatisfied ☐

Totally dissatisfied ☐

Figure 7.5   A balanced rating scale

Who are you going to vote for at the next election?

Some people will reply

I don't know.

If the interviewer then pressures respondents to provide a definitive answer, so that eventually, to bring the interview to a close, the respondent nominates one of the political parties, that would not be acceptable research. 'Don't know' is a valid response.

So, strictly speaking, you should have a middle option, but you do not need to worry about everybody ticking it. It is a myth that everybody makes a beeline for the middle option as though it is an easy option and saves them from having to think. They do tend to put what they think and you do get a range of answers. Respondents do sometimes avoid the extremes of the scale. So if it looks as though the scores are clustered around the middle, it is probably not because respondents are aiming for the middle but because they are avoiding the extremes. Of course, that can be a problem if you have used only a 5-point scale, because if some respondents avoid the extremes they only have three points left to choose between. However, there are many other issues to consider when selecting the most appropriate type of rating scale, and these will be examined in the next chapter.

Questionnaire layout

- ■ Instructions
- ■ Opening questions
  - ● Present – past
  - ● Behaviour – attitude – classification
- ■ Question sequence
  - ● Involvement process
  - ● Topic groupings
- ■ Layout
  - ● Space
  - ● Colour

Figure 7.6   Questionnaire design – the layout

Figure 7.6 outlines some of the key issues to consider when planning the layout of your questionnaire.

INSTRUCTIONS

The first thing respondents will see on the questionnaire will be the instructions. These must be totally clear. If a questionnaire can be filled in wrongly you can be sure that some respondents will do so. Therefore you must have very clear instructions, even if that means that they take up quite a lot of space. You can find examples of instructions in the sample questionnaires in the appendices to this book.

OPENING QUESTIONS

After the instructions, the questionnaire will move into the first questions. These should be as easy as possible. Many people will make a quick judgement when they see a questionnaire about how long it is going to take to fill in. That judgement will be based on a combination of how long the questionnaire is and how difficult the questions are. The difficulty of the questions might be determined by glancing at the first couple of questions, so it is always a good idea to make them as easy as possible.

In that respect, the present is easier for people than the past, and behaviour (what we do) is easier than attitude (what we think about things), so the ideal topic for the first two questions would concern present behaviour – things we do now. For example, before moving into complex questions about people's attitudes towards their electricity supply, a regional electricity company might start with a very simple behavioural question such as:

Which of the following electrical appliances do you have in your home?

Kettle
Television
etc.

It is not unusual to start with two or three questions on issues of little or no importance to the company simply in order to give respondents an easy start to the questionnaire. However, there is an obvious trade-off here with length, so if the questionnaire is already quite long, the easy opening questions may have to be sacrificed for the sake of brevity. For example, if a questionnaire already covers four sides of A4 paper, it would not be advisable to extend it to a fifth solely in order to add some easy but unimportant questions at the beginning.

Classification questions should come at the end. Some people may be offended by what they see as impertinent questions about age, occupation or income, so it is always better to leave classification questions until after the other questions. The one exception here would be quota samples, where respondents have to be qualified before their inclusion in the survey.

QUESTION SEQUENCE

As far as CSM questionnaires are concerned, there will be a list of fifteen to twenty customer requirements that have been identified in the exploratory research, and they will have to be rated for importance as well as satisfaction. So you should list the requirements and first rate them all for importance, then list them again and rate them all for satisfaction. But in what order should the requirements be listed? Strictly speaking, they should be listed in random order and preferably not in the same order on every questionnaire, on the grounds that the earlier questions might influence respondents' thinking on the later ones. Therefore, for really accurate research, the list of attributes should be rotated.

However, it would not be common practice to print ten different versions of a customer survey questionnaire so that the questions can be rotated. In reality, most commercial research would just print one version, with the questions in the same order on every questionnaire. There are two basic choices relating to which order the questions should be in. One option is to base the order on the sequence of events that customers typically go through when dealing with your company. This works very well for one-off events like taking out a mortgage or making an insurance claim. However, for many organisations that have ongoing relationships with customers, with a variety of contacts for different things at different times, using the 'involvement process' as a basis for question sequencing will not work. In that situation it would be usual to use topic groupings, with all the questions on quality grouped together, all the questions on delivery together and so on.

LAYOUT

The main issue here is the trade-off between length and layout. Of course you do not want your questionnaire to look too long, but it will look even worse if it is too cluttered, making it look as though it will be very difficult to fill in. So questions should be spaced out, with an attractive layout, even if it makes the questionnaire run into more pages. Use of colour is also worthwhile. Even a two-colour questionnaire can appear much more attractive: semi-tones can be used very effectively for clarification and differentiation. Although printed in only one colour in this book, and on smaller pages (they would have been A4 in real life), the sample questionnaires in the appendices will give some idea of how semi-tones can be used to clarify the rating scales.

8 RATING SCALES

The third key aspect of questionnaire design is the rating scale, and since CSM is about measuring satisfaction and the rating scale is the tool used to do the measuring, it is the most critical aspect of questionnaire design for CSM. Hence the devotion of a separate chapter to the topic. Figure 8.1 shows five of the most commonly used rating scales for CSM. The Likert scale and verbal scale are similar in that they both use words to describe the points on the scale. The SIMALTO scale, sometimes called a fully descriptive verbal scale, also uses words but its format is very different. The numerical scale, as expected, uses numbers for the rating and the ungraded scale provides no labels for the points on the scale, only the extremes.

Before moving on to an assessment of the different scales and their advantages and disadvantages for CSM purposes, Figures 8.2 to 8.6 provide sample questionnaires using each of the scales. You may wish to fill them in so that you can experience them for yourself before reading the assessment of the scales. The scales in Figures 8.2 to 8.5 each have a definite number of points, but in reality (apart from the ungraded scale, which is an unlabelled continuum) any scale can, in theory, have any number of points and any scale can have a mid-point or no middle option, depending on whether it has an odd or an even number of points.

---

1 Likert scale

Typically degrees of agreement with a statement

2 Verbal scale

Verbal satisfaction and importance ratings

3 SIMALTO scale

Simultaneous multi-attribute trade-off or fully descriptive verbal scale

4 Numerical rating scale

Marks out of 5, 10 or 100 and so on

5 Ungraded scale

Attitude battery between bi-polar extremes

Figure 8.1   Rating scales

There are two sections to each sample questionnaire because you always have to measure importance as well as satisfaction. So when you are filling them in, you should complete the first section on importance according to how important or unimportant to you each point is. For the second section on satisfaction you will have to think of a specific occasion or supplier and score your satisfaction with that organisation.

Please read the following statements and place an X in the box which most accurately reflects how much you agree or disagree with the statement or put your X in the N/A box if it is not relevant to you.

	N/A	Agree strongly	Agree slightly	Neither agree nor disagree	Disagree slightly	Disagree strongly
1 When at the supermarket it it is important to be able to park the car with ease	❑	❑	❑	❑	❑	❑
2 When at the supermarket it is important that there is a wide range of merchandise	❑	❑	❑	❑	❑	❑
3 When at the supermarket it it is important that the checkout queues are short	❑	❑	❑	❑	❑	❑

Below are some features of shopping at _____.
Please place an X in the box which most accurately reflects
how much you agree or disagree with the statement or put your X in the N/A
box if it is not relevant to you.

	N/A	Agree strongly	Agree slightly	Neither agree nor disagree	Disagree slightly	Disagree strongly
1 There are plenty of car park spaces	❑	❑	❑	❑	❑	❑
2 There is a wide range of merchandise	❑	❑	❑	❑	❑	❑
3 The checkout queuing time is short	❑	❑	❑	❑	❑	❑

Figure 8.2   Likert scale

Below are some features of supermarket shopping.
Please place an X in the box which most accurately reflects
how important or unimportant each feature is to you or put your cross in
the N/A box if it is not relevant to you.

	N/A	Very important	Quite important	Neither important nor unimportant	Quite unimportant	Very unimportant
1 Ease of parking	☐	☐	☐	☐	☐	☐
2 Choice of merchandise	☐	☐	☐	☐	☐	☐
3 Queue times at the checkout	☐	☐	☐	☐	☐	☐

Below are some features of shopping at _____.
Please place an X in the box which most accurately reflects
how satisfied or dissatisfied you are with each item or put your cross in
the N/A box if it is not relevant to you.

	N/A	Very satisfied	Quite satisfied	Neither satisfied nor dissatisfied	Quite dissatisfied	Very dissatisfied
1 Ease of parking	☐	☐	☐	☐	☐	☐
2 Choice of merchandise	☐	☐	☐	☐	☐	☐
3 Queue times at the checkout	☐	☐	☐	☐	☐	☐

Figure 8.3   Verbal scale

Using the table below, please show what levels of service you think a supermarket should provide by marking appropriate boxes according to the following key:

U = unacceptable level of service – *mark all boxes which show an unacceptable level of service*

E = expected level of service – *mark only one box on each row*

I = ideal level of service – *mark only one box on each row*

You can place more than one letter in one box

(*eg* if the level of service you expect is unacceptable).

If the item is not relevant to you, place an X in the N/A box.

	N/A	Level 1	Level 2	Level 3	Level 4	Level 5
1 Ease of parking	☐	Never any spaces in the car park	Rarely any spaces available	Spaces available but hard to find	Usually a lot of spaces available	Always lots of spaces available
2 Choice of merchandise	☐	There is hardly any choice	There is a limited choice	There is a fairly good choice	You can get almost anything you want	You can always get everything you want
3 Queue times at checkout	☐	16+ minutes	10–15 minutes	6–9 minutes	3–5 minutes	1–2 minutes

Using the table below, show the levels of service you believe to be provided by the supermarket by placing an X for supermarket XXX and a Z for supermarket ZZZ in the appropriate boxes.

Please mark one box on each row for each supermarket. It does not matter whether you mark the same or different boxes for each supermarket.

If the item is not relevant to you, place an X in the N/A box.

	N/A	Level 1	Level 2	Level 3	Level 4	Level 5
1 Ease of parking	☐	Never any spaces in the car park	Rarely any spaces available	Spaces available but hard to find	Usually a lot of spaces available	Always lots of spaces available
2 Choice of merchandise	☐	There is hardly any choice	There is a limited choice	There is a fairly good choice	You can get almost anything you want	You can always get everything you want
3 Queue times at checkout	☐	16+ minutes	10–15 minutes	6–9 minutes	3–5 minutes	1–2 minutes

Figure 8.4   SIMALTO scale

Below are some features of supermarket shopping. Using the key
below, please circle the number which most accurately reflects how
important or unimportant each feature is to you or circle
N/A if it is not relevant to you.

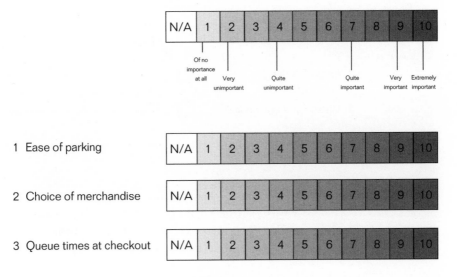

1 Ease of parking

2 Choice of merchandise

3 Queue times at checkout

Below are some features of shopping at _____.
Using the key below, please circle the number which most accurately
reflects how satisfied or dissatisfied you are with each item or circle
N/A if it is not relevant to you

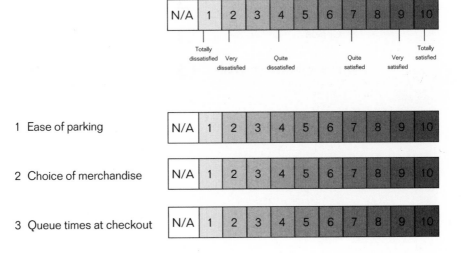

1 Ease of parking

2 Choice of merchandise

3 Queue times at checkout

Figure 8.5 Numerical scale

Below are some features of supermarket shopping. Please place an X at the point on the line which most accurately reflects how important or unimportant each feature is to you or place an X in the N/A box if it is not relevant to you.

	N/A	Extremely important		Extremely unimportant
1 Ease of parking	☐	├─────────────────────────┤		
2 Choice of merchandise	☐	├─────────────────────────┤		
3 Queue times at checkout	☐	├─────────────────────────┤		

Below are some features of shopping at _____.
Please place an X at the point on the line which most accurately reflects how satisfied or dissatisfied you are with each item or place an X in the N/A box if it is not relevant to you.

	N/A	Extremely satisfied		Extremely dissatisfied
1 Ease of parking	☐	├─────────────────────────┤		
2 Choice of merchandise	☐	├─────────────────────────┤		
3 Queue times at checkout	☐	├─────────────────────────┤		

Figure 8.6 Ungraded scale

An assessment of the scales

THE LIKERT SCALE

Very common in many types of attitude research, the Likert scale is easy to fill in but does have the considerable disadvantage that the bold statement may bias respondents' answers. Likert scales on satisfaction questionnaires are always positively biased. You very rarely see negatively biased ones using examples of appalling service for the bold statements. (such as '*The restaurant was filthy . . . Agree – Disagree*'). Bias is even more likely on importance questions where the respondent is effectively being told '*It is important that . . .*'

THE VERBAL SCALE

This verbal alternative remains easy to complete: is much more neutral and has the distinct advantage of incorporating the concepts being measured (importance and satisfaction), thus reducing the risk of respondent confusion. We feel that the verbal scale is the simplest and clearest (and therefore likely to be the one most accurately completed with the least error) of the three verbal-type scales.

THE SIMALTO SCALE

The SIMALTO scale is not easy to fill in and for that reason would not typically be used on a self-completion questionnaire. It is most effective in personal interview situations where the interviewer, who knows how to complete the questionnaire, can use show cards to guide respondents through the options. With considerably more difficulty it can be used in telephone interviews in business markets if the respondent is sent the range of answers by post or fax before the interview. The obvious advantage of the SIMALTO scale is the precision of the information generated. It is the only scale that can be directly linked to service standards and is therefore most applicable to service-intensive situations such as travel, banking or helplines. It is also good for comparisons between different types of expectation or the performance of different suppliers. However, it is also the most complex and expensive methodology and, for most companies, should only be used if an agency is conducting the survey.

There is also doubt over its suitability for measuring satisfaction. As stated earlier, the SIMALTO scale is ideal for measuring the supplier's adherence to a set of service standards, but that provides a measure of organisational performance rather than a measure of satisfaction.

NUMERICAL SCALE

Numerical scales are easy to fill in and easy to analyse. They also make it possible to have a wider scale. It is not practical to have many points on a verbal-type scale and this is a considerable disadvantage since the differences between satisfaction survey results from one period to the next will often be very small. A wider scale enables the respondent to be more discriminating, especially at the satisfied end of the scale, which is important since it is only the very satisfied who are likely to remain loyal. Unlike most other scales, the numerical scale can be used whatever the method of data collection. Possibly the most powerful argument in favour of the numerical scale is its user-friendliness when it comes to analysing and, very important, communicating the results to colleagues in your organisation. The simple average scores generated by the 10-point numerical scale are easy for everyone to understand and paint a very clear picture of the results and their implications. This will be seen in the simple charts in Chapter 10, showing results derived from numerical scales which clearly illustrate the areas to address, compared with the far less graphic frequency distributions which must be used for analysing results from verbal-type scales. This is an extremely important factor in favour of using numerical scales for CSM questionnaires because internal feedback is where the CSM process fails in many organisations. There is simply insufficient company-wide understanding of the areas where service-improvement efforts should be focused. Having clear and simple results from the survey, which all staff can immediately understand, is the essential starting point in this battle for hearts and minds.

UNGRADED SCALE

The ungraded scale appeals to visually oriented respondents. If a series of questions is completed in a column, the marks on the line provide a good visual impression of the relative importance (or satisfaction) for the list of attributes. The least cluttered, it introduces the least bias, but some respondents find its lack of benchmarks disconcerting, and to analyse it accurately a scanner must be used. If the questionnaires are scanned, the results can be classified using any number of points on the scale – 5, 10 or even 100. Unfortunately, the scanner is undoubtedly assigning the scores to the 100-point scale with considerably more accuracy than the respondent applied when placing the original mark on the line on the questionnaire. Ungraded scales can be useful for questionnaires that need to be completed very quickly (for example at the point of sale), but are not widely used for measuring satisfaction.

Conclusions

On balance we feel that the 10-point numerical scale is the most suitable for measuring satisfaction. The verbal scale is probably the easiest to complete, but is far less suitable at the analysis and feedback stage. The SIMALTO scale provides the most precise and extensive information and is ideal for monitoring adherence to service standards, but is very costly and not totally suitable for measuring satisfaction. The Likert and ungraded scales should not be used for CSM.

9 INTRODUCING THE SURVEY

As we stated when we looked at maximising response rates, the introductory letter has a very important role to play. As well as increasing the response rate it should also improve the quality of response by raising the perceived value of the exercise in customers' minds. Carrying out a customer survey also provides an opportunity to enhance the image of your organisation by demonstrating its customer focus, and the introductory letter will play an important role here. Conversely, carrying out a customer survey in an amateurish or thoughtless way could damage your reputation. Figure 9.1 summarises the three main aspects of introducing the survey and these concern whom to tell, how to tell them and what to tell them.

1 Whom to tell
  - Everybody in the sample
  - All customers

2 How to tell them
  - Visits
  - Personalised mailing
  - Existing customer communications

3 What to tell them
  - Why they should take part
  - How they will take part
  - What they will be told afterwards

Figure 9.1   Introducing the survey

Whom to inform

If you are serious about the CSM process there is only one answer to this question. You should inform all customers. Making sure that all customers know that you are committed to customer satisfaction and are prepared to invest to achieve it is a significant factor in making satisfaction gains. Instead of sitting back and hoping that customers will notice your efforts and commitment, you should take control and make sure they do.

How to inform them

This will clearly depend on how many customers you have. If you have a very small number of customers in a business market it is most productive to explain the process personally to each one through well-briefed customer contact staff. However, with even a medium-sized customer base and a more selective programme of customer visits this could become very costly, but a personal letter to each one would be quite feasible. With a very large customer base a special mailing would be costly, although it is worth considering its long-term effectiveness in building customer loyalty compared with a similar spend on advertising. If cost does rule out a special mailing you should at the very least use existing communication channels to inform customers of your CSM programme. This may include printing a special leaflet to be enclosed with an existing mailing or creating space in an existing customer publication such as a newsletter.

What to tell them

There are three things you need to tell them:

- Why you are doing it
- How you are going to do it
- The feedback you will provide afterwards.

THE PURPOSE OF THE SURVEY

Don't assume that customers will correctly interpret the purpose of a CSM survey. Many people confuse surveys with selling approaches. Others correctly distinguish research from selling but may see all research as a brain-picking exercise which benefits the supplier rather than the customer. It is therefore essential to communicate successfully that the main beneficiary of the CSM process is the customer. It may seem obvious, but point out that the purpose of the survey is to identify whether customers' requirements are being fully met so that action can be taken to improve customer satisfaction where necessary.

THE SURVEY DETAILS

Customers clearly need to know what form the survey will take. If the introductory letter accompanies a postal questionnaire it will include the instructions for completing and returning the questionnaire. If you undertake a telephone survey an introductory letter should give brief details of the topics that will be covered and should stress that an appointment will be made to interview customers at a time convenient to them. It is also useful at this point to reiterate how valuable the customer feedback is, in order to encourage the highest possible participation rates.

FEEDBACK

Research evidence suggests that promising feedback is the single most effective element in increasing response rates. The introductory letter should therefore inform customers that they will receive feedback on the survey results and on the key issues that have been identified as a result of the survey. You should also promise to share with customers the actions that you plan to take to address any issues. More details on the form this customer feedback should take will be provided in Chapter 13.

A sample introductory letter is shown in Figure 9.2.

Dear————

As part of our ongoing commitment to customer service at XYZ Ltd, we are about to conduct a survey to measure customer satisfaction. I would therefore like to enlist your help in identifying those areas where we fully meet your needs and those where you would like to see improvements. We attach the utmost importance to this exercise since it is your feedback which will enable us to continually improve our service in order to meet your needs.

I believe that this process needs to be carried out in a professional manner and have therefore appointed The Leadership Factor Ltd, an agency which specialises in this work, to carry out the exercise on our behalf. They will contact you in the near future to arrange a convenient time for a telephone interview lasting approximately 15 minutes.

Your responses will be treated in total confidence by The Leadership Factor and we will receive only an overall summary of the results of the interviews. Of course, if there are any particular points that you would like to draw to our attention, you can ask for them to be recorded and your name associated with them if you wish.

After the survey we will provide you with a summary of the results and let you know what action we plan to take as a result of the findings. I regard this as a very important step in our aim of continually improving the level of service we provide to our customers and I would like to thank you in advance for helping us with your feedback.

Your sincerely

XXXXX
Chief Executive

Figure 9.2 Introductory letter for the main survey

10 ANALYSING THE RESULTS

In this chapter we will cover the various analytical techniques used for CSM surveys, in particular looking at how to analyse the results for different types of rating scales, and we will explain how to calculate a customer satisfaction index. The explanations in this chapter are accompanied by charts to illustrate the outcomes. Any data included in the charts and tables is fictitious and does not apply to any specific organisation.

CSM surveys are not usually difficult to analyse. A good spreadsheet such as Microsoft Excel or Lotus 123 would perform all the statistical analyses required to produce the results shown in this chapter. Specialist analytical software is available. The most commonly used in the research industry are SPSS, Snap and Pinpoint. Unless you are carrying out a large number of surveys it will probably not be cost-effective to go beyond a spreadsheet, particularly if people in your organisation are already competent at using one of the spreadsheets.

What matters most

Assuming the use of a 10-point numerical scale, the first thing respondents will have been asked to do in a CSM survey is to rate the importance to them of a list of customer requirements by giving each one a score out of 10 where 10 would mean extremely important and 1 would mean of no importance at all. The hypothetical example used to illustrate the results is from a typical supermarket survey. For clarity, only eight attributes are shown in the chart whereas in real life there would usually be fifteen to twenty customer requirements included on the questionnaire. Figure 10.1 shows the simplest way to report the results. The scores given here are the average (that is, the arithmetic mean) scores out of 10 given by the respondents for each of the attributes.

The chart clearly demonstrates what matters most to customers. Average importance scores above 9 indicate that the requirement is extremely important to customers. Those scoring above 8 are important and above 7 they are quite important. It is unusual to generate many average importance scores below 7 in the main survey because only those items shown by the

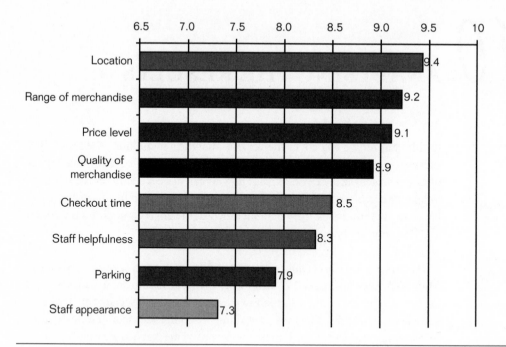

Figure 10.1   Importance scores

exploratory research to be important to customers should find their way on to the questionnaire. It is interesting that in the surveys that we undertake for clients, attributes scoring only 5 or 6 for importance usually did not feature strongly in the exploratory research results but were included in the main survey at the request of the client, often because the client felt that they must be important to customers. Such attributes rarely score any higher for importance at the main survey stage across a much larger sample. Suppliers often do not understand their customers as well as they think they do!

Two additional points should be noted about the chart shown in Figure 10.1. First, everything is listed in order of importance to the customer. It does not matter in what order the attributes were listed on the questionnaire. There is an important message for everybody here:

'These are the things that are important to customers and this is the order of priority'.

You should remain consistent and list everything in order of importance to the customer all the way through reporting the results.

Second, the scale on the chart does not go from 1 to 10. If it did, all the bars would appear at first glance to be of a very similar length and anybody who just skimmed the CSM report might glance at it and conclude:

'That's not telling us anything; there's not much difference there.'

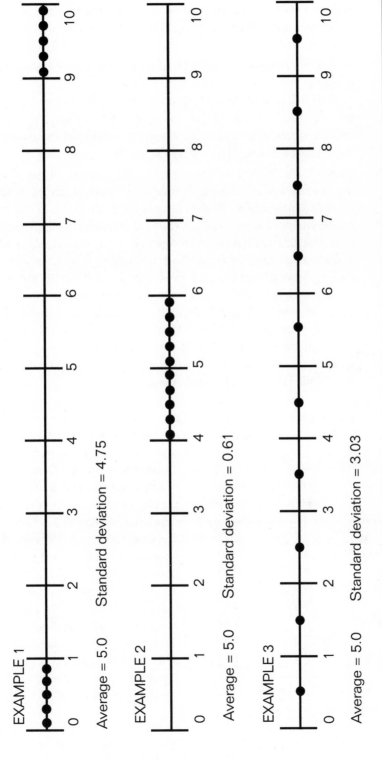

Figure 10.2 Varying data producing the same average score

In reality there is a big difference in importance between an average score of 7 and one of 9. So it is always better to truncate the scale to highlight the differences and make sure you get the message across.

It is not necessary to undertake a large amount of complex statistical analysis to get the main results you need from a CSM survey. However, there is one analysis that should always be carried out whenever an average score is shown. This is the standard deviation, which tells you what lies behind the average scores, as averages can sometimes mask wide variations in the meaning of the data, as shown by Figure 10.2.

The average score in the three examples is identical, yet the conclusions from that hypothetical survey would be completely different. In Example 1, the ten people surveyed are divided into two equal groups of people who hold diametrically opposed views. In Example 2, there is a strong consensus of opinion with all the ten respondents giving very close scores. In Example 3 the respondents' views are evenly spread across the entire spectrum. This is not apparent from the average scores but can be seen in the standard deviation, which effectively shows the average distance that all the scores are away from the overall average. There is a statistical formula for the standard deviation, but these days nobody would calculate it manually. Any spreadsheet or statistical software would display the standard deviation for a set of data, just as it would show the average.

Figure 10.3 shows the standard deviations for the importance scores shown in Figure 10.1. On a 10-point scale, a standard deviation of around 1 or below indicates that there is a strong consensus of opinion. Store location, for example, is extremely important to almost all the people surveyed. On the other hand a standard deviation of 2 or above demonstrates a wide disparity of views. Looking at parking, some respondents must have scored 8s, 9s and 10s for importance, whereas others must have scored very low. In that example it is not difficult to understand why those scores might occur. Some people travel to the supermarket by car and for most of them ease of parking is very important. Others travel on foot or by bus and for them it is not important at all.

	Importance score	Standard deviation
Location	9.4	0.71
Range of merchandise	9.2	0.83
Price	9.1	0.79
Quality of merchandise	8.9	1.02
Checkout time	8.5	1.14
Staff helpfulness	8.3	1.37
Parking	7.9	2.25
Staff appearance	7.3	1.76

Figure 10.3   Importance scores with standard deviations

Sometimes, however, the reason for a high standard deviation might not be so obvious. In such circumstances you would need to look behind the average score and find out the cause of the disagreement. Let's say there was a high standard deviation for the importance of staff helpfulness. In that eventuality, you could break down the data, look at the scores given by the different segments and perhaps find that staff helpfulness is extremely important to older people who expect a high level of personal service, but that it is not particularly important to younger people who expect everything to be self-service.

What we do best

After scoring the list of requirements for importance, respondents would be asked to score the same list for satisfaction. Figure 10.4 shows the average scores for satisfaction. You can see that they are still listed in order of priority to the customer and still with the truncated scale to highlight the differences.

Average satisfaction scores above 9 on a 10-point scale show an extremely high level of customer satisfaction. Scores of 8 equate to 'satisfied' customers, 7 to 'quite satisfied' and 6 (which is only just above the mid-point of 5.5) to

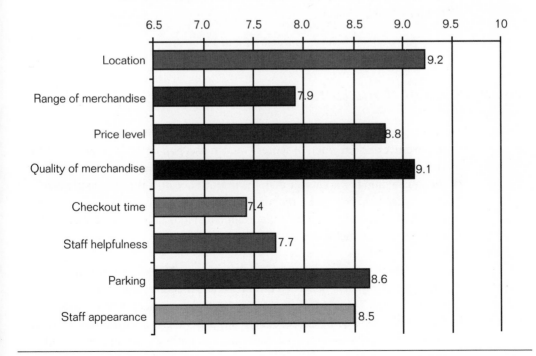

Figure 10.4 Satisfaction scores

'borderline' or 'much room for improvement'. Average satisfaction scores of 5 or lower are below the mid-point and suggest a considerable number of dissatisfied customers. Any attribute with an average satisfaction score below 7 should be treated seriously. It would also be good practice in telephone surveys to probe any scores below 6 out of 10 to find out why the low score was given. This will enable the research to explain any poor satisfaction scores such as 'checkout time' or 'staff helpfulness'. Self-completion questionnaires can ask for comments about low satisfaction scores, but not all respondents will provide them and they will often be quite brief.

As before, standard deviations should be calculated for each satisfaction score because behind an apparently satisfactory score may be a group of customers who are extremely satisfied but some who are very unhappy. If so, you need to understand which types of customers are not being satisfied by your organisation. This may be determined by examining the scores for different segments, which helps to explain why you need a sufficiently large sample to provide statistically reliable sample sizes at segment level.

The satisfaction chart provides very interesting information, but the most useful outcomes can be produced when you put the importance and the satisfaction scores together and ask that very simple but absolutely fundamental question,

Are we doing best what matters most to customers?

Doing best what matters most

The answer to that question is to be found in Figure 10.5. By comparing the importance and satisfaction scores you can use 'gap analysis' to identify PFIs (priorities for improvement). Not rocket science, gap analysis indicates that if the satisfaction bar is shorter than the importance one, the company may have a problem! But that is the main strength of the chart. It is clear, simple and obvious. Anybody in the organisation can look at it, understand it and draw the right conclusions.

Clearly there are some areas, such as 'location and 'quality of merchandise,' where the company concerned is more or less meeting customers' requirements. There are some, such as 'staff appearance', where customers' requirements are being exceeded. (*Note*: Remembering the implication of the high standard deviation for the importance of parking, the supplier would be prudent not to assume it is exceeding customers' requirements on that attribute without checking the satisfaction scores for parking provided by the

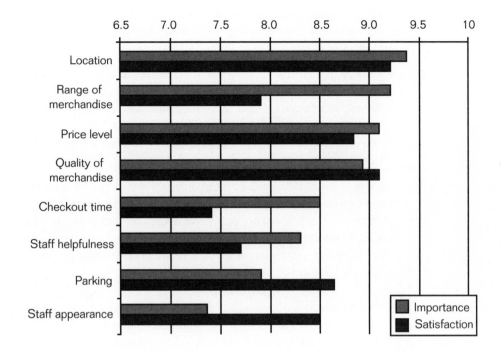

Figure 10.5   Gap analysis to highlight PFIs

segment that thought parking was very important). Most significant, there are some attributes where the company is falling short and these are the ones it needs to focus on if it wants to improve customer satisfaction. These are the PFIs, the priorities for improvement. The bigger the gap, the bigger the problem, and you can see from Figure 10.5 that the biggest PFI, the area with the greatest potential for improving customer satisfaction, is not the attribute with the lowest satisfaction score (quick checkout) but the one with the largest gap – range of merchandise.

However, there are other factors to consider when deciding what the PFIs should be.

Determining the PFIs

We would say that on a 10-point scale any gap above 1 is significant and gaps in excess of 2 are serious, but by definition, it is not feasible to have too many *priorities* for improvement. In deciding which gaps are the most serious and should be adopted as PFIs, four factors should be considered.

1 **Size of gap**   The most important factor is the size of the gap. Normally a greater gain in customer satisfaction will be achieved by closing a large gap rather than a small gap.

2 **Importance to customers**   Almost as significant as the size of the gap is the importance of the issue to customers, whose satisfaction judgement is more heavily influenced by their most important requirements. Closing a slightly smaller gap on something that is a top priority to the customer may therefore generate more satisfaction gain than addressing a larger gap on an issue of lower importance.

3 **Quick wins**   Some PFIs will be more difficult, more time-consuming and more costly to address than others. We are certainly not advocating avoidance of the difficult issues but we do believe it is important to adopt at least one PFI which can be addressed relatively easily – a quick win. It is very helpful if both customers and employees can see prompt action being taken as a direct result of the survey.

4 **Policy/regulations**   Some organisations may be constrained from closing some gaps by circumstances beyond their control, such as regulations, or by a deliberate corporate strategy which is contrary to customers' wishes. In our supermarket example it would not be feasible to move the supermarket in the near future even if customers were dissatisfied with 'convenience of store location'. Another example is that a company whose strategy is to be a premium-priced supplier may choose not to close a gap on price. Either of these positions is perfectly valid, but in both cases the supplier would have to work particularly hard to close any remaining gaps to give customers enough reason to go the extra mile to the less convenient location or to pay the price premium.

Business impact

However important customer satisfaction is, it cannot be bought at any price. Ultimately, the decision to invest in customer satisfaction improvement has to be a trade-off between the cost of making those improvements and the potential gain from doing so. To clarify that business impact decision it is helpful to plot the potential satisfaction gain against the cost and difficulty of making the necessary improvements. A business impact matrix for the supermarket is shown in Figure 10.6.

The most positive business impact will be made by adopting PFIs that will generate the greatest possible gains in customer satisfaction at the lowest possible cost. Based on categorising customer requirements into three broad

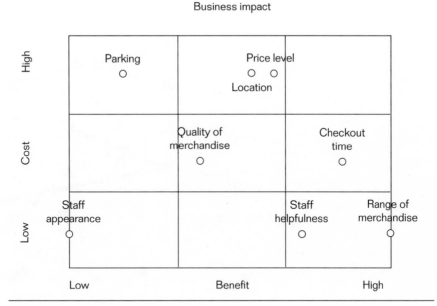

Figure 10.6   Business impact matrix

bands according to the cost and difficulty of making improvements, the business impact matrix illustrates where the most cost-effective gains can be made. As shown in the matrix, some requirements, particularly those in the cells in the bottom right-hand corner, such as range of merchandise and staff helpfulness, should bring high returns due to their large satisfaction gaps, and relatively low cost. However, requirements in the top left-hand corner, such as parking, would bring little benefit, due to low or non-existent satisfaction gaps and high relative cost.

Performance profiles

We will now move on and look at how some of the other scales would be analysed. A performance profile, as shown in Figure 10.7, would often be used to show the results of an ungraded scale.

On the left, the chart shows five of the attributes measured in the survey. The solid line shows respondents' importance scores, the dotted line shows their level of satisfaction with Company A and the dashed line shows how satisfied they are with Company B. At first glance you may find that it is not very easy to figure out what it all means and which company is doing better. In fact, Company A is the more successful at satisfying customers because its satisfaction profile tracks the customers' importance scores. Company A is doing best what matters most to customers. Company B is very good at some

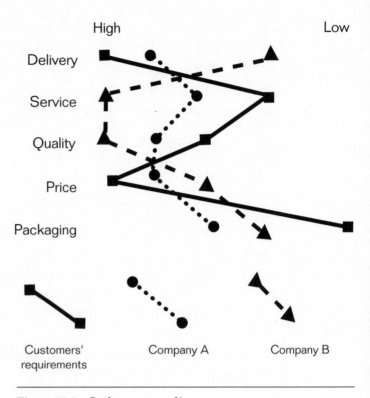

Figure 10.7   Performance profiles

things but it is good at the wrong things. It is best at meeting the requirements which matter least to customers.

Once you have tuned in to a performance profile chart it tells you all you need to know. You can look at the gaps between importance and satisfaction and identify the PFIs. However, it is not as clear or as simple as the earlier bar chart and, of course, there would not just be five attributes on the questionnaire but more likely fifteen to twenty, so the profiles would be more extensive than those shown in Figure 10.7, making it even more difficult to interpret. Such considerations are extremely important, because if staff throughout the organisation do not understand the CSM results and therefore do not take them on board, it is very unlikely that much action will be taken to improve customer satisfaction. So it is very important at the outset of your survey to ask:

If we do the survey in this way, how will we display the results?

It is crucial that you end up with results in a form that everybody will be able to understand easily. If you commission a survey from an outside agency you should also ask them the above question right at the beginning or you may find that your results are delivered in the form of performance profiles.

Frequency distributions

If verbal-type scales are used for questionnaires, the results must be analysed using a frequency distribution – in other words, how many people said what. A frequency distribution is shown in Figure 10.8. The numbers are usually percentages, so in the example shown, 34 per cent are very satisfied with the opening hours, 27 per cent are quite satisfied. It is a totally accurate summary of the results, but it does not make a very strong impression.

Attribute	Very satisfied	Quite satisfied	Neither satisfied nor dissatisfied	Quite dissatisfied	Very dissatisfied
Opening hours	34	27	6	21	12
Car parking	16	26	28	23	7
Queuing time	4	18	48	19	11
Friendliness of staff	32	34	23	10	1
Appearance of staff	40	44	16	0	0

Figure 10.8   Frequency distribution

It would be possible to produce charts for individual attributes, each with five bars showing varying levels of satisfaction or importance by attribute. However, the real problem is the absence of a single average score for each attribute. For example, it is not possible to make a direct comparison between the importance score for opening hours and the satisfaction score for opening hours, so you cannot carry out a gap analysis to arrive at the PFIs. That is a major disadvantage of using a verbal-type scale, what you can do with the results is very limited compared with the numerical scale.

Some people look at the data they get from verbal-type scales, recognise the limitations and realise that it would be much more useful to have average scores. They then immediately solve the problem by changing the points on the verbal scale into numbers and carry on as though they had used a numerical scale from the outset. People change 5-point verbal-type scales into various numerical scales as shown in Figure 10.9.

Verbal scale	Numerical scale (1)	Numerical scale (2)
Very satisfied	5	+2
Quite satisfied	4	+1
Neither satisfied nor dissatisfied	3	0
Quite dissatisfied	2	−1
Very dissatisfied	1	−2

Figure 10.9 Changing verbal into numerical scales

The numerical data in Figure 10.9 illustrate one of the problems. Once you decide to change the information given to you by the customers into something else, what do you change it into? The two sets of numbers shown in the table will not give the same result. Even if everybody standardised on the 5–4–3–2–1 scale, how can you be sure that a customer who responded 'quite satisfied' would have scored 4 on the numerical scale? As a general rule, it should never be the researcher's role to change any answers provided by respondents. However, there is an even bigger problem caused by changing verbal responses into numerical scales. It is not statistically valid, as illustrated by Figure 10.10.

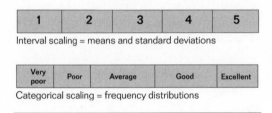

Interval scaling = means and standard deviations

Categorical scaling = frequency distributions

Figure 10.10 Interval and categorical scaling

Strictly speaking, a numerical scale is known as interval scaling and it is statistically valid to average the scores given by customers because all the points on the scale assume roughly equal proportions in the respondent's mind. With a verbal-type scale, strictly called a categorical scale, the points on the scale do not assume equal proportions in respondents' minds, as shown in Figure 10.10. For that reason it is only considered to be statistically valid to analyse a categorical scale using a frequency distribution like the one shown in Figure 10.8.

The satisfaction index

After you have identified the PFIs, the second major outcome to be produced is an overall index of customer satisfaction, often called a satisfaction index or a customer satisfaction index. There are several possible ways of producing such an index. You could include a catch-all question at the end of the questionnaire such as:

And overall, how satisfied are you with the products and services of . . . ?

Or

And overall, how satisfied are you with your experience of . . . ?

The trouble with this approach is that the more variables you ask people to consider when responding to a question, the less reliable the answer is, and there are a great many variables in that overall satisfaction question. On reflection, you do not need to ask the catch-all question because you have already asked each respondent about all the main things that make them satisfied or dissatisfied. A second approach would therefore be to calculate the overall average of all the satisfaction scores. That would be better, but it would not be ideal, because some things are more important to customers than others, and their most important requirements influence their satisfaction judgement more than things that are less important to them. An accurate satisfaction index therefore has to work in the same way. It has to be more strongly influenced by the attributes with the highest importance scores. In other words it must be a weighted average satisfaction score, which requires a two-step process for its calculation.

CALCULATING THE WEIGHTING FACTORS

The importance scores are used to calculate the weighting factors. The first column of data in Figure 10.11 shows the average importance scores from the supermarket example. To calculate the weighting factors simply total all the importance scores. In this example they add up to 68.6. Then express each one as a percentage of the total. Using 'staff appearance' as an example, 7.3 divided by 68.6, multiplied by 100 produces a weighting factor of 10.64 per cent.

Attribute	Importance scores	Weighting factors
Store location	9.4	13.70%
Range of merchandise	9.2	13.41%
Price level	9.1	13.27%
Quality of merchandise	8.9	12.97%
Checkout time	8.5	12.39%
Staff helpfulness	8.3	12.10%
Parking	7.9	11.52%
Staff appearance	7.3	10.64%
Total	**68.6**	

Figure 10.11 Calculating the weighting factors

CALCULATING THE SATISFACTION INDEX

The second step is to multiply each satisfaction score by its corresponding weighting factor. The first column of data in Figure 10.12 shows all the average satisfaction scores and the second column shows the weighting factors that were calculated in Figure 10.11. Taking staff appearance as the example again, the satisfaction score of 8.5 multiplied by the weighting factor of 10.64 per cent produces a weighted score of 0.9. The overall weighted average is determined by adding up all the weighted scores. In this example they add up to 8.41, so the supermarket's weighted average satisfaction score is 8.41 out of 10. It is normal to convert that score into a percentage and say that the satisfaction index is 84.1 per cent.

Attribute	Satisfaction score	Weighting factor	Weighted score
Location	9.2	13.70%	1.26
Range of merchandise	7.9	13.41%	1.06
Price	8.8	13.27%	1.17
Quality of merchandise	9.1	12.97%	1.18
Checkout time	7.4	12.39%	0.92
Staff helpfulness	7.7	12.10%	0.93
Parking	8.6	11.52%	0.99
Staff appearance	8.5	10.64%	0.90
Weighted average			8.41%
Satisfaction index			**84.1%**

Figure 10.12 Calculating the satisfaction index

In this example, the satisfaction index shows that the supermarket is 84 per cent successful in satisfying its customers. To demonstrate the mathematical basis of the formula, imagine that the supermarket was such a wonderful supplier that all the customers surveyed insisted on giving satisfaction scores of 10 out of 10 for every single one of the customer requirements. In that eventuality the average satisfaction scores would all be 10. The weighting factors would all stay the same because they come from the importance scores, and the weighted scores in the right-hand column of Figure 10.12 would all be different to each other, but they would all add up to precisely 10.0. That is how the formula works. Total customer satisfaction on all their requirements would produce a satisfaction index of 100 per cent.

UPDATING THE SATISFACTION INDEX

In Chapter 2, we said the satisfaction index had to be updateable. It must provide you with a comparable measure of satisfaction that you can monitor in the years ahead even if the questions on your questionnaire have to change as customers' requirements change. Basically, the satisfaction index answers this question:

> How successful are we at satisfying our customers according to the twenty things that are most important to them? (Assuming twenty attributes on the questionnaire.)

If the questionnaire has to change in the future because customers' priorities have changed, the satisfaction index remains a measure of exactly the same thing:

> How successful are we at satisfying our customers according to the twenty things that are most important to them?

That comparability also applies to organisations with different customer groups who need to be asked different questions in the same year. Provided that the exploratory research has been correctly undertaken, the satisfaction indexes from two or more surveys asking different questions are directly comparable.

11 BENCHMARKING YOUR PERFORMANCE

Since satisfaction indexes are directly comparable (provided the correct methodology has been followed), it is perfectly feasible to compare performance across a large number and a wide variety of organisations. Our company has a large database of CSM results, enabling us to continually update a 'league table' which puts any individual result into context against other organisations.

So what about the performance of our supermarket achieving a satisfaction index of 84.1 per cent? Is it any good? Actually, it is very good, as shown in Figure 11.1, which gives an overview of the range of scores achieved by different organisations. The figure of 84 per cent is well above average.

The league table ranges from a very small number of excellent organisations which can achieve a satisfaction index of 90 per cent, down to a low of around 55 per cent. The median score (the mid-point) is around 80 per cent, so a satisfaction index in the 80s is above average, and under 80 per cent it is below average compared with organisations generally. It may also be interesting to make comparisons with organisations in your own sector. How do you compare with other manufacturers or other retailers?

Even more important than whether your satisfaction index is above or below average is why you are in that position. Part of the answer will be found in your comparison against other organisations at an individual attribute level. There may be one key attribute where your performance is weaker than that of other organisations. Figure 11.2 shows how a fictitious company compares against the average scores of all other organisations across each of the attributes on its questionnaire.

Increasingly it is recognised that only the best is good enough, so you need to be able to benchmark your organisation against the best for each attribute, not just the average, as shown in Figure 11.3.

Satisfaction Index™ League Table

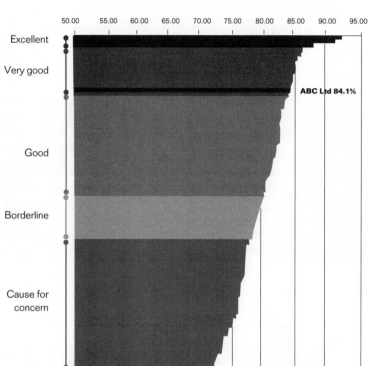

Figure 11.1   Satisfaction benchmark league table

Our company, The Leadership Factor, can provide satisfaction benchmark comparisons. Details of this service are provided in Appendix 4.

Comparisons with direct competitors

To make comparisons with direct competitors you need to collect your own data by extending the scope of your CSM survey. There are two main ways of generating the comparisons.

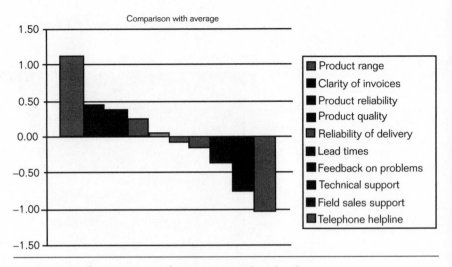

Figure 11.2 Comparative performance at attribute level

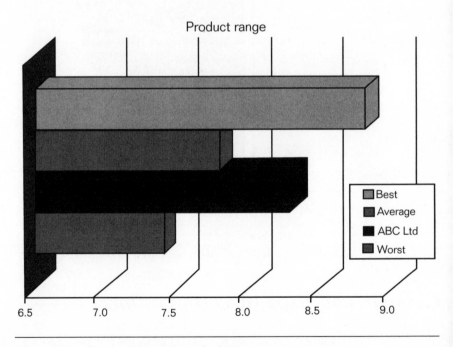

Figure 11.3 Benchmarking against the best

COMPARISON INDICATOR

A simple and effective way of gaining an understanding of your position against competitors is to add a basic question to your questionnaire, such as:

Compared with similar stores/restaurants/venues/hotels that you visit, would you say that XYZ Ltd is:

- The best
- Better than most
- About the same as most
- Worse than most
- The worst?

This will provide the type of data shown in Figure 11.4, which can form the basis for a very clear 'comparison indicator' to monitor over the years.

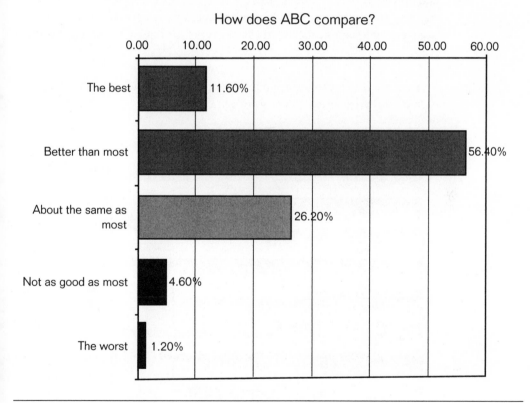

Figure 11.4   General comparison indicator

MARKET STANDING

Gaining more precise information on how you compare with direct competitors can only be acquired by extending your CSM study into a full market standing survey. This exercise differs in two ways from the process described in this book. First, the sample frame (the population from which the sample is drawn) must comprise all the buyers of the product or service in question and not just your own customers or even your own contacts. Clearly, to get a reliable view of how you compare against competitors you must survey all shades of opinion, from your best friends to your worst enemies. Acquiring, or, if necessary, compiling such a comprehensive sampling frame is critical for the subsequent validity of the exercise and can be a lengthy process.

Second, the satisfaction section of the questionnaire must be extended to generate scores for all the suppliers with whom that respondent is familiar. Not all respondents will be able to give scores for all competitors, so you will end up with different sample sizes for each one. Consequently, for a market standing survey a larger sample size is almost always necessary since you need a reliable sample for the smallest competitor against whom you want a reliable comparison.

From the data you can make a direct comparison with all competitors across each customer requirement, as shown in Figure 11.5.

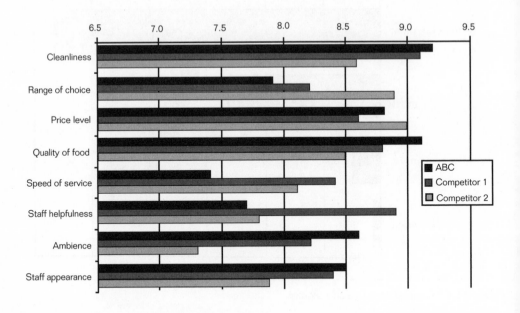

Figure 11.5 Competitor comparisons at attribute level

Using the same process as described for calculating the satisfaction index, you can work out the weighted average satisfaction scores for each supplier and produce a market standing chart as shown in Figure 11.6.

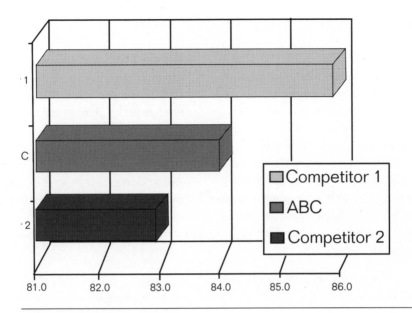

Figure 11.6 Market standing

Clearly, the market standing survey provides extremely useful competitor intelligence but the research to produce it reliably will be considerably more extensive and expensive than a survey of your own customers. Moreover, even with the more detailed data generated by a market standing survey, the wider comparisons against other organisations described in the early part of this chapter remain important, for two reasons. First, customers will often form their judgement of your organisation by comparing you with the full range of organisations that they deal with, not just with your direct competitors (with whom they may have no dealings). Second, even if a market standing survey heralds you as better than your direct competitors, you may be operating in a market where all the suppliers are delivering a relatively poor level of service.

Achieving customer satisfaction

Customer satisfaction is measured frequently. Sampling is extensive. Surveys are quantitative as well as qualitative (i.e. delivery times and feelings count equally); the measures are taken very, very seriously. They are reviewed unfailingly by top management: the development of such measures is taken as seriously as the development of budgetary measures or product reliability measures. Evaluation of people in all functions at all levels is significantly affected by the satisfaction measures.

Tom Peters, *A Passion for Excellence*

Figure 11.7 Top US companies and customer satisfaction

Why the difference

- Top management support
- Prominence
- Accurate methodology
- Extensive feedback
- Swift decision making
- Action
- Continuing focus

Figure 11.8 Characteristics of companies achieving high levels of satisfaction

Knowing how you compare against other organisations on overall customer satisfaction and on performance at attribute level provides an essential basis for making improvements but it still does not explain why some organisations are more successful than others at making those improvements and achieving a high level of customer satisfaction. A very strong clue was provided by Tom Peters in *A Passion for Excellence*. A relevant passage from the book is shown in Figure 11.7.

Our experience from working with a large number of organisations on customer satisfaction has highlighted several characteristics that are shared by the most successful ones. These are summarised in Figure 11.8.

TOP MANAGEMENT SUPPORT

The first and most important characteristic of organisations near the top of the satisfaction benchmark league table is a very high level of top management support and commitment. They do not just pay lip service to customer satisfaction but make it quite clear from their actions that satisfying customers really is the top priority of their organisation. This is most clearly demonstrated when difficult budgetary decisions have to be taken. Are additional resources made available to provide extra staff when the customer survey shows a problem with service levels, or does top management simply encourage customer contact staff to try harder?

PROMINENCE

In companies where customer satisfaction is a top priority, the customer survey process and the results are given very high prominence throughout the organisation. All possible methods of communication are used to provide information about the CSM process, including e-mail, staff newsletters, team briefing, notice boards, large posters on walls and special workshops.

ACCURATE METHODOLOGY

Organisations that are serious about customer satisfaction use the most accurate methodology they can when measuring it. You will not find them conducting a postal survey and ignoring the problem of non-response bias if they get low response rates. You will not find them drawing conclusions from ridiculously small sample sizes. You will not find them using their own members of staff (such as salespeople) to interview customers whom they know personally. A measure of customer satisfaction that is of dubious reliability is probably worse than no measure at all. Successful companies realise this and are prepared to invest in a robust methodology.

EXTENSIVE FEEDBACK

Companies at the top of the league table are not afraid of sharing their customer satisfaction results with customers as well as with employees. They know that providing extensive internal feedback is the essential precursor to effective staff involvement in the service improvement process. They also understand that customers' attitudes change only slowly, even when customer service is improving, so that process must be accelerated by giving customers information on improvements that have been made. Providing feedback is probably one of the biggest differentiators between the better and poorer performing suppliers and will be covered in Chapter 13.

SWIFT DECISION MAKING

Once a customer survey has been completed, all the information required to make decisions on improving customer satisfaction is available. No more will emerge by delaying things. On the contrary, customers' expectations may be changing and their satisfaction will certainly be declining if problems remain unresolved. The most effective organisations build decision making into their CSM project plan. They schedule a senior management meeting within days of the survey completion date and a process for cascading those decisions (often along with wider feedback of the survey results) a few days later.

ACTION

Clearly, all the measuring, the reporting, the decision making, and the feedback must then lead to action. The whole point of conducting a CSM survey is to improve customer satisfaction, and that will be achieved only through taking action on the PFIs. At least the use of a good CSM methodology will provide incontrovertible evidence about what the PFIs are. However, some organisations are far more effective at taking action than others. This is not a book on how to implement management decisions, but the ability to do so is an important differentiator between organisations at opposing ends of the satisfaction benchmark league table.

CONTINUING FOCUS

Senior management must beware of adhering religiously to the first six steps in this section and then moving their attention on to other things. Improving customer satisfaction is very much 'a journey not a destination', and the company must be constantly moved along that journey. If staff know that something is important to top management they will give it more priority, so it is up to senior managers, starting with the chief executive, to keep the spotlight on the service improvement programme and continually reiterate its importance to the organisation. One very tangible way of doing this is to include customer satisfaction as a key element of staff reward and appraisal strategies. As indicated by the quotation from Tom Peters in Figure 11.7, customer satisfaction related pay has been relatively common in the USA for some years. In the UK it is still in the domain of the early adopter organisations, so, for the time being at least, its introduction remains as a competitive advantage opportunity for UK organisations seeking leadership positions.

12 THE INTERNAL SURVEY

While carrying out a customer survey it can be extremely beneficial to survey employees at the same time as customers to identify 'understanding gaps' – areas where staff do not properly understand what is important to customers or fail to realise that the level of service they provide is not good enough. This exercise is known as an internal survey and it involves administering a slightly modified version of the customer questionnaire to employees. Exactly the same attributes should be measured but you will effectively ask your staff:

> How important or unimportant do you think these things are to our customers?

and:

> How satisfied or dissatisfied do you think customers are with our performance in these areas?

An internal survey is normally based on a self-completion questionnaire which should be given out to and collected from employees to achieve the highest possible response rate. By highlighting understanding gaps the internal survey may help to pinpoint the causes of any customer dissatisfaction. A sample questionnaire for an internal survey is shown in Appendix 3.

Understanding customers' requirements

Using the same results for the supermarket that we saw earlier, the chart in Figure 12.1 shows the difference between the customers' average score for the importance of each attribute and the average score given by employees. Alarm bells should sound when employees underestimate the importance of a customer requirement. The chart shows that employees significantly underestimate the importance of checkout time, scoring it 0.7 lower than customers.

Understanding customer satisfaction

The second internal survey chart, shown in Figure 12.2, indicates the difference in average scores for satisfaction given by customers and

Importance scores

Figure 12.1 Customers' requirements – the internal view

employees. There may be a problem where employees overestimate their success in satisfying customers. The chart shows that they do this with checkout time. The average satisfaction score given by employees was 1.2 higher than that given by customers. It is easy to imagine the kind of understanding gap that could occur here. The employees may be completing the questionnaire and thinking:

> We're pretty good on checkout time. As soon as there are four customers in a line, we rush over and open a new till.

Meanwhile, customers in the stores are thinking:

> What dreadful service. There are already three people in this queue and they still haven't opened another checkout.

As well as highlighting understanding gaps on specific attributes, an internal survey will sometimes highlight a much deeper malaise in the organisation. Whilst some organisations have an incredibly accurate understanding of customers' needs and perceptions, others can display a woeful misunderstanding across the board. In these latter cases, the internal survey has identified a significant staff training need since the organisation will never

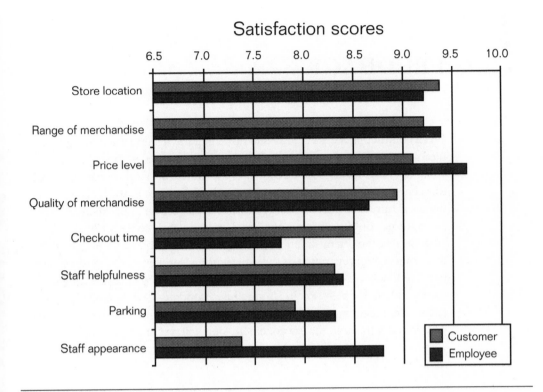

Figure 12.2 Customer satisfaction – the internal view

satisfy its customers until staff understand what they must do to achieve customer satisfaction. Sometimes, when employees give satisfaction scores that are consistently higher than those given by customers, a degree of unhealthy complacency can be diagnosed. However, the opposite can also happen, where employees give significantly lower satisfaction scores than customers for all the attributes. This can be a sign of poor staff morale, sometimes based on too many years of criticism by management for their poor performance.

Even if the internal survey does not identify any understanding gaps or highlight any wider problems within the organisation, completing the questionnaires is a very tangible way of involving employees in the CSM process and making them think about the issues of importance to customers. Once the results have been analysed, employees find it most interesting to compare their scores with those given by customers and that added interest helps to facilitate the internal feedback process. It is this topic that we turn to in the next chapter.

13 FEEDBACK

From conducting a CSM study and obtaining the results to achieving the ultimate objective of an improvement in customer satisfaction, a lengthy chain of events has to occur. Known as the satisfaction improvement loop, this chain is illustrated in Figure 13.1. Each of the steps in the loop is a potential hurdle at which the organisation's satisfaction improvement programme could stumble. Although there are clearly some major issues surrounding the organisation's ability to make and implement decisions following the survey, much of the satisfaction improvement loop is concerned with feedback. It also has implications for the frequency of conducting a survey. There is little point in conducting an update survey to monitor your success in improving customer satisfaction if there is only a slim chance that your journey through the improvement loop will be complete. This explains why many organisations conduct surveys annually or, at most, every six months.

Figure 13.1   The satisfaction improvement loop

Two audiences need informing about the results of a CSM survey – the customers and the employees. Both are of equal importance, although the ways and timing of providing the feedback will differ. This chapter will first review the internal feedback process before moving on to discuss alternative ways of providing feedback to customers.

Internal feedback

Feeding back the results to employees is an essential element in the long-term health of a CSM programme. Little action will be taken to improve customer satisfaction if employees don't know enough about the results or their implications. The extent of the feedback provided to employees will also send messages about how important the customer survey is to the organisation. So rather than providing superficial feedback through newsletters, notice boards or e-mail, the results should be personally presented in the form of feedback workshops, preferably to all employees but at least to all those who have an important role in delivering customer satisfaction. For larger organisations, face-to-face feedback workshops for all or a significant proportion of employees will be quite a costly exercise. Therefore, if some people in the organisation question the wisdom of that investment, it is not difficult to quantify the cost of the workshops in terms of staff pay or lost production. Any opponents of the feedback workshops can then be asked whether improving customer satisfaction is worth that investment to the organisation. With a little more difficulty it would be possible to calculate the extent to which customer loyalty would have to increase to justify that investment, and you will find, almost without exception, that the required increase would be extremely small.

A suggested agenda for an internal feedback workshop is shown in Figure 13.2. The workshop should start by demonstrating that the survey was professionally conducted and therefore provides a reliable measure – in short, that the right questions were asked of the right people. The exploratory research which led to the design of a suitable questionnaire, plus the robustness of the sample, should be explained. The results should then be presented – the importance ratings, the satisfaction ratings, the gap analysis and the satisfaction index. Explain how the index is calculated and what it means; otherwise it will be perceived as little more than another dubious number invented by management. As suggested in Chapter 11, it is also helpful to put the satisfaction index and the individual satisfaction scores in context and demonstrate to employees how their performance compares with that achieved by other organisations.

1 Questionnaire
 • exploratory research

2 Sampling
 • representative of customer base
 • random – without bias

3 Survey results
 • importance ratings
 • satisfaction ratings
 • gap analysis
 • satisfaction index

4 Ideas for action
 • short-term
 • long-term

Figure 13.2   Internal feedback

Finally, you should look to the future. Start by reiterating the importance of the PFIs and then take the opportunity to invite ideas about how they might be addressed. Time permitting, it is very useful to break employees into small groups to discuss the issues. Ask them to brainstorm ways in which the PFIs could be addressed. Once a list of ideas has been generated, they should be sorted into two categories: those which could be implemented easily, quickly and at low cost (the quick wins); and those that are longer-term, on grounds of cost or difficulty. Employees should then select the ones they consider to be their three best short-term and three best long-term ideas, and be prepared to present their suggestions to the rest of the workshop. This will result in a large number of ideas for action. The selection process can be taken a step further by asking everybody to score the full list of ideas in order to identify the best overall short-term and long-term ideas. Apart from the fact that employees, who are close to the action, will often think of good ideas which would not have occurred to management, the great advantage of this approach is that employees are far more likely enthusiastically to embrace a service improvement programme which they have helped to shape rather than one which has simply been handed down by management.

Feedback to customers

Having promised feedback to customers in the introductory letter, you must now provide it. You therefore need to consider three things:

• Which customers should receive feedback?
• What information is to be provided?
• How will it be communicated?

WHICH CUSTOMERS?

At the very least, feedback should be provided to all customers who took part in the survey. If the survey was an anonymous self-completion survey, you will not know who returned the questionnaires, in which case it will not be possible to target feedback to respondents. If an agency has carried out the survey, respondent confidentiality can be assured without anonymity, so the agency will know which customers have responded and should receive feedback. A second possibility is simply to provide feedback to all customers in the sample, whether or not they responded, but if feedback is to be provided to non-respondents in the sample, why not to customers generally? For organisations with a very large customer base the obvious answer is 'cost'. As with internal feedback, the pertinent question is whether the 'cost' can be justified by the benefit.

Stimulating customer attitude change

Many organisations fail to realise the potential value of feeding back the CSM results to the entire customer base. The satisfaction improvement loop shown in Figure 13.1 demonstrates that before you can achieve gains in customer satisfaction, customers must first notice any improvements made by your organisation and second, modify their attitudes accordingly. Both of those steps are major hurdles to overcome. As far as the first is concerned, many organisations take it for granted that if they make improvements along the lines indicated by the customer survey customers will notice. That is a very dangerous assumption. Most customers will have far more important things on their mind than looking out for changes made by supplier organisations. They will often fail to notice changes. Those they do notice will often be by chance, and probably only after repeated exposure. Once customers have noticed the changes, they will still have to modify their attitudes before they will feel more satisfied, and certainly before they will communicate that increased satisfaction to anyone else. Clearly, the more you can do to accelerate that process, the more effective your CSM programme will be. Providing feedback on the survey results and on the actions your organisation plans to take in response to the customers' views is a good step in the right direction. By working on the satisfaction improvement loop, you can, to an extent, 'talk up' customer satisfaction. Indeed, as we will see later in this chapter, where there are perception gaps, talking up customer satisfaction is the only way to improve it. Consequently, there is an opportunity to improve customers' perception of your organisation by providing information on the survey results to the entire customer base.

WHAT INFORMATION?

The starting point is to produce a short feedback report containing the information which will be provided to customers. This should include a summary of the results, followed by an outline of the key issues arising from the survey. The key issues will usually be the PFIs, but it is unwise to refer to them as PFIs in the feedback report since the terminology might suggest that your organisation has too much improving to do! 'Key issues' or 'survey outcomes' is therefore more suitable wording. Having communicated the results, you need to tell customers what action will be taken as a result of their feedback and when it is going to be taken. This may seem a bold commitment, but if the goal is to improve customer satisfaction, action will have to be taken anyway. Informing customers that it is going to be taken is the first step in improving their perception and accelerating the satisfaction improvement loop.

One of the most difficult decisions for organisations to take is the level of detail to go into when providing feedback on the survey results to customers. One option is to feed back the results exactly as they are, showing the average importance scores together with the average satisfaction scores, as shown in Figure 13.3.

Figure 13.3 Accurate feedback

Some organisations feel very uneasy about providing the actual scores, perhaps through fear that they may fail to improve the following year or, in some close-knit industrial markets, that the information might fall into the hands of a competitor. To alleviate such concerns, an alternative is to provide indicative feedback, using symbols or general descriptions to suggest levels of satisfaction (see Figure 13.4)

	Customer requirement	Satisfaction
1st	Location	☺
2nd	Range of merchandise	☹
3rd	Price	☺
4th	Quality of merchandise	☺
5th	Checkout times	☹
6th	Staff helpfulness	☹
7th	Parking	☺
8th	Staff appearance	☺

Figure 13.4 Indicative feedback

Although it is understandable why some organisations worry about feeding back the exact scores, indicative feedback can be more damaging. Symbols and general descriptions will often look worse than the real scores, as is the case with Figures 13.3 and 13.4. Moreover, if customers form the conclusion that the results have been massaged in an attempt to disguise poor performance, their impression of the organisation could be adversely affected.

HOW WILL IT BE COMMUNICATED?

How the information is provided depends mainly on the size of the customer base. Personal presentation is by far the most effective method and is quite feasible for companies with a fairly small number of key accounts. For a medium-sized customer base, a copy of the feedback report should be mailed with a personalised letter. If very large numbers of customers are involved, mass market communications will need to be used. These might include a company newsletter or a brief survey report mailed with another customer communication such as a bill. Retailers and other organisations whose customers visit them can cost-effectively utilise point-of-sale material. This may include posters, leaflets, display cards or stands. Moreover, customer contact staff can be briefed to support the feedback drive through their verbal communications with customers. Point-of-sale displays might, for example, encourage customers to ask staff for further details. Even TV advertising has been used to communicate to very large customer bases the survey results and the fact that action is being taken.

Progress reports

The final hurdle of the satisfaction improvement loop is the fact that even after they have noticed your improvements, customers still have to change their attitudes before a satisfaction gain is achieved. Although people can form attitudes quickly, they tend to change them slowly, but it is possible to speed up customers' attitude change and improve satisfaction by providing updates on action that has been taken, preferably at least twice between annual surveys.

Perception or reality

There is still one more reason for providing customer feedback and progress reports. Where organisations receive poor satisfaction scores for individual attributes, these may be explained as a 'performance gap' or a 'perception gap'.

As an illustration, imagine a company received a poor average satisfaction score for 'on-time delivery'. This could be a 'performance gap', meaning that they really are very poor at delivery – they do not keep their delivery promises, they are always arriving late and always letting customers down. That would be a performance gap, and in that situation the only way the company would be able to increase customer satisfaction would be to improve its delivery performance.

On the other hand, it might have received a poor average satisfaction score for 'on-time delivery' and yet know that its delivery performance is very good. The company might even monitor it and have computer print-outs showing delivery reliability at 98.7 per cent this month, 99.2 per cent last month and so on for the last year. Perhaps the company went through a bad patch about two years ago when it installed its new computer system and experienced some real delivery problems then. The problem may have been resolved soon afterwards, but not in the customers' minds! Customers can remember bad things that suppliers do to them for a very long time, and if improvements are made, but customers' attitudes remain focused on the bad times, you end up with 'perception gaps'.

If the company has a perception gap, it can't improve customer satisfaction by improving its performance. In the 'on-time delivery' example, that has already been done. It can improve satisfaction only by demonstrating to customers how good its performance really is and consequently hope to change their attitudes. That is a communications task and illustrates why customer feedback is so important. The customer feedback straight after the survey can start the process. In the example quoted, the company could acknowledge 'on-time delivery' as a key issue arising from the survey and tell customers that it is taking the matter very seriously and will report back on progress on a regular basis. (Needless to say, the company would not tell its customers that they were wrong!)

We have seen many cases of perception gaps and how they have been successfully overcome by customer feedback. One company in an industrial market had exactly this type of perception gap for on-time delivery. They informed customers that they were going to set targets for delivery reliability, monitor their performance against those targets every month and feed back the results to customers. (In fact, they were already monitoring the delivery reliability, but it doesn't do any harm for customers to think that this measure had been introduced as a result of the customer survey).

Every month for the next year they sent a fax to each customer, plotting the delivery reliability against target and highlighting how many of the customer's own deliveries that month were on time or late. Since delivery reliability had already been improved, the customers' faxes would show 100 per cent reliability for their own deliveries almost every month. One year later, when the customer survey was updated, the score for on-time delivery had improved significantly even though the delivery performance had not changed at all!

14 SATISFACTION, DELIGHT AND LOYALTY

A question that we are sometimes asked by senior managers from all kinds of organisations is:

> Customer satisfaction is all very well, but does it make any difference?

It always strikes us as absolutely incredible that anybody in a senior position in a business can ask such a question. The obvious response is:

> Does it make any difference to your behaviour as a customer whether you are satisfied or not?

Intuitively, based simply on our own customer behaviour, we all know that there is a link between customer satisfaction and loyalty. If we are not satisfied we will go elsewhere. In some markets it is much more difficult, time-consuming or costly to change supplier than in others, but the trend is towards supplier switching becoming easier, and even in the most difficult markets the principle still applies. If you make customers dissatisfied you will erode their loyalty.

Nevertheless, it is still not unusual to come across statements such as:

> Customer satisfaction is old hat! Where it's at now is . . . delighting the customer . . . or . . . customer loyalty . . . or . . . customer value management . . . or even . . . 'wowing' the customer.

The originators of such glib statements rarely pause to analyse the difference between customer satisfaction and their own well-packaged alternative, so let's try to do just that.

As we said at the beginning of this book, few people would disagree that the concepts shown in Figure 14.1 will contribute to business success, but how, in what proportions and what is the difference between them? As a first step towards clarification we can immediately remove one of the concepts. For most organisations, the notion of 'delighting the customer' is at best a total irrelevance and at worst a positive danger.

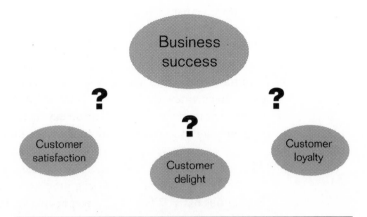

Figure 14.1   Keeping customers – some concepts

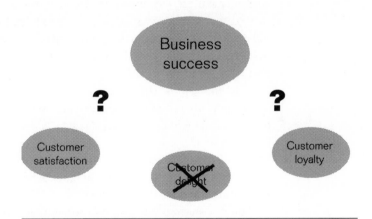

Figure 14.2   Customer delight is irrelevant

Customer delight seems very credible. People say things like:

> In today's competitive markets customer satisfaction is no longer enough; you have to *delight* customers, give them something they didn't expect to keep their business.

It sounds good at conferences and reads well in books. But what, precisely, do organisations in various markets actually do to delight the customer and give them something they did not expect? And how do you keep on doing it, because presumably you will not just delight the customer merely by continuing to provide the same service, however good it is? It is also interesting to ask yourself how many times you have been a 'delighted customer'. Do you use only suppliers that consistently delight you? We suspect not, because for most organisations, the prospects for 'delighting' their customers are virtually non-existent (see Figure 14.2).

We concede that there are exceptions. If you take your children to Florida you may well all be delighted as a family with your day's experience in the Magic Kingdom. But what about paying your electricity bill, visiting your local convenience store for groceries, spending an evening in the pub, withdrawing money from your savings account, ordering stationery for the office, having new tyres fitted to your car? Are you wowed and delighted after every customer experience? Do you expect to be? Do you cross that supplier off your list if they haven't wowed you? We think not.

The vast majority of organisations providing everyday products and services stand absolutely no chance of delighting customers even once, let alone on a continuous basis. Where the concept can even become dangerous is that in focusing management time and effort on desperately trying to come up with yet another gimmick to wow the customer the organisation may be taking its eye off the much more fundamental, but admittedly less sexy objective of customer satisfaction. We know from conducting hundreds of customer surveys that there are virtually no organisations capable of completely satisfying their customers, let alone consistently delighting them. Even the best organisations usually have failings in a few areas and most organisations are falling significantly short of satisfying customers in a number of basic ones. Even for those organisations where delighting the customer is not an irrelevance, they should still be focusing their efforts on mastering walking before enrolling in the running classes.

Delight is therefore merely an extension of satisfaction. We are obviously not saying that it is wrong, or a bad thing, to delight customers. Of course it is a good thing when a customer is delighted. Therefore, if you can identify delighted customers and pinpoint something specific that delighted them, you should clearly try to do more of it. However, for many organisations that will be a difficult and costly process. Finite resources will usually be more productively focused on customer satisfaction research and improvement issues.

In short, unless you have very satisfied customers, which most organisations do not, the gains are to be made from solving the problems that are causing customer dissatisfaction, in other words, addressing the PFIs. Even for the best organisations, delighted customers are no different to extremely satisfied customers. Consistently meeting their requirements and providing the highest standards of customer service will make them very satisfied/delighted, whichever terminology you prefer. But will it keep them loyal?

Satisfaction and loyalty

At the beginning of this book, customer loyalty was shown as the middle link of the chain in the business performance model between customer satisfaction and business success. Establishing the relationships between those three links is most easily done by starting at the end of the chain because the link between customer loyalty, or customer retention, and profitability is already widely accepted (see Figure 14.3).

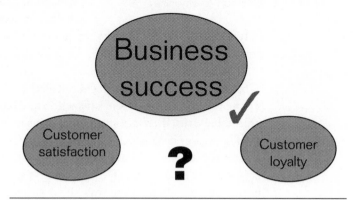

Figure 14.3   The loyalty–profitability link is accepted

It has been demonstrated many times that increasing customer retention boosts profits. This is mainly because it is far less costly to keep existing customers than to win new ones. High rates of customer decay therefore have to be countered by high sales and marketing spend to attract new customers unless the organisation is to shrink in size. Conversely, if customer decay is reduced but the rate of customer acquisition is maintained, the company will grow. And how do you increase customer retention and reduce customer decay? The answer is simple. By increasing customer satisfaction. Apart from being intuitively sound, and, we are sure, conforming with your own experience as a customer, there is a growing body of third-party evidence to support the assumption. There are now increasing numbers of companies (mainly in the USA) which have been measuring customer satisfaction for some years. Many have linked CSM scores with their customer database, enabling them to plot the subsequent behaviour of customers who have taken part in customer surveys. The critical question, of course, is whether customer who have given high scores in CSM studies show greater subsequent loyalty than those giving lower scores, and the answer is a resounding yes, they do. This was demonstrated by the chart we showed at the beginning of the book (Figure 1.2 on page 3) which is well worth revisiting as we approach the end.

Customer's stated level of satisfaction	Loyalty rate
Excellent/very satisfied	95%
Good/satisfied	65%
Average/neither satisfied nor dissatisfied	15%
Poor/quite dissatisfied	2%
Very poor/very dissatisfied	0%

Figure 14.4   Satisfaction–loyalty links

Clearly the relationship is not linear. The relationship between satisfaction and loyalty climbs steeply as customer satisfaction increases and is at its strongest at the highest levels of satisfaction (see Figure 14.4). Evidence from companies using numerical scales is very similar. They also show a strong positive correlation between satisfaction and loyalty. Generally, an overall satisfaction score of 60 per cent results in only about 35 per cent loyalty, but an overall satisfaction score over 80 per cent overall results in over 90 per cent loyalty.

What is particularly interesting about all these figures is that there is not only a close relationship between satisfaction and loyalty, but also in the critical 'mid-table' area, there are substantial gains in loyalty to be made from quite small increases in satisfaction. We have very many organisations in our *Satisfaction Benchmark* database whose satisfaction index is hovering around or just below 80 per cent. They can expect significant gains in loyalty not from inventing gimmicks to wow the customer but from addressing their basic PFIs and improving overall customer satisfaction by perhaps just two or three percentage points.

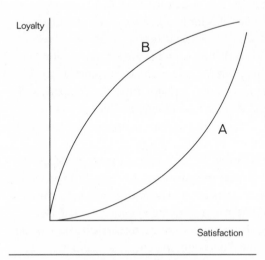

Figure 14.5   Satisfaction–loyalty links in different markets

It must be noted, however, that there is no satisfaction–loyalty ratio which applies as a norm across all markets. In some markets (typically very competitive ones with high levels of supplier switching), loyalty will rise steeply only at the highest levels of satisfaction, as shown by curve A in Figure 14.5. In other markets, with higher levels of customer inertia or stronger barriers to supplier switching, customer satisfaction may fall much lower before loyalty is significantly eroded, as shown by curve B. It is clearly useful to know which type of curve is more applicable to your organisation, and for this, you will need to develop your own model.

Modelling and forecasting

Having gathered the trend data and established the satisfaction–loyalty ratio in your market for your organisation, you can start to build models. Some companies now have 'business performance models' based on their CSM results that have quantified the precise links between customer satisfaction, customer loyalty, sales and profit. They know how much a 1 per cent improvement in customer satisfaction will improve loyalty and how much that will contribute to profits. Clearly, this is a very powerful forecasting tool.

ISS (International Service System, the biggest service company in the world) has gone one step further and produced a model based on several years' employee satisfaction measurement as well as CSM data. Their work shows a clear linear relationship between employee satisfaction and customer satisfaction. Based on weighted indices from its 5-point numerical scale, their model shows that a unit change in employee satisfaction results in a very similar change in customer satisfaction.

These conclusions have been supported by other organisations such as McDonalds, whose employee surveys have demonstrated that the outlets with the most satisfied staff achieve the highest sales and profits figures. Further supporting evidence for the link comes from MORI, whose research shows that 41 per cent of employees who are 'very satisfied' with their job will 'recommend their company without being asked', whereas 31 per cent of those 'dissatisfied' with their job will 'talk unfavourably about the employer's products/services without being asked'. So the future of business performance modelling clearly lies in the integration of employee satisfaction and customer satisfaction data to develop an extremely powerful forecasting tool (see Figure 14.6).

At the moment, most organisations outside North America are a long way from developing such models because they do not possess the trend data which form the essential base, but that will change as satisfaction measurement, especially CSM, is becoming increasingly widely adopted. Our final conclusion returns to the core topic of this book. We have outlined a step-by-step guide to measuring customer satisfaction professionally. Many customer surveys are still far from professional and they will not produce a reliable result. Even to make the right management decisions now about improving customer satisfaction a professional approach is important. If you want to progress to the kind of business performance modelling shown in Figure 14.6, an accurate measure is absolutely essential.

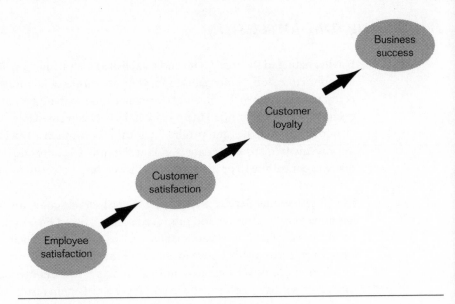

Figure 14.6 Business performance modelling – the future

APPENDIX 1   SELF-COMPLETION QUESTIONNAIRE

ABC Ltd Customer Survey: Self-completion

INTRODUCTION AND GUIDANCE

The purpose of this survey is to find out what you expect from ABC Ltd as a supplier and how satisfied or dissatisfied you are with the service you receive. We need everyone to answer the questionnaire very honestly, and to encourage this, The Leadership Factor guarantees to protect the identity of everyone who completes it, in accordance with the Market Research Society Code of Conduct.

The questionnaire is divided into two main sections (A and B). Both sections cover the same topics, but in Section A we want to know **how important or unimportant each item is to you**, and in Section B, **how satisfied or dissatisfied you are** with ABC's performance on each topic.

Please complete the questionnaire and return it in the pre-paid envelope to The Leadership Factor Ltd by **[date]**.

How to complete Section A
In this section, we would like you to score how important or unimportant various issues are to you.

Some issues may be more important than others, and we want to get a good idea of your priorities. So, first of all, read through all the questions before deciding which is the most important one. Then score the level of importance out of 10 using the following scale.

1	2	3	4	5	6	7	8	9	10

Of no importance at all   Not particularly important   Moderately important   Important   Very important   Extremely important

Score your most important issue first, then score the rest in that section.

For example, look at Question 1, 'On-time delivery'. If on-time delivery is your most important requirement you should circle box number 10 as shown.

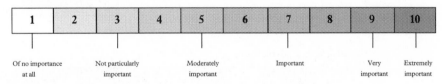

1. On-time delivery   N/A | 1 | 2 | 3 | 4 | 5 | 6 | 7 | 8 | 9 | ⑩

Then score the remaining items in the list using the same scale. If you feel that an issue is not relevant to customers, or you have no direct experience of what is being asked, you should tick the box marked 'N/A'.

SECTION A: IMPORTANCE

How important or unimportant are the following issues to you as a customer of ABC?

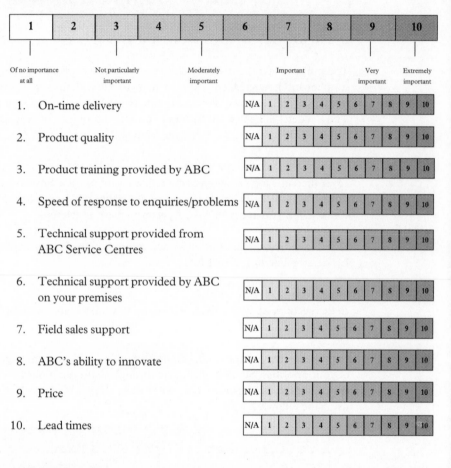

| 1 | 2 | 3 | 4 | 5 | 6 | 7 | 8 | 9 | 10 |

Of no importance at all · Not particularly important · Moderately important · Important · Very important · Extremely important

1. On-time delivery   N/A 1 2 3 4 5 6 7 8 9 10

2. Product quality   N/A 1 2 3 4 5 6 7 8 9 10

3. Product training provided by ABC   N/A 1 2 3 4 5 6 7 8 9 10

4. Speed of response to enquiries/problems   N/A 1 2 3 4 5 6 7 8 9 10

5. Technical support provided from ABC Service Centres   N/A 1 2 3 4 5 6 7 8 9 10

6. Technical support provided by ABC on your premises   N/A 1 2 3 4 5 6 7 8 9 10

7. Field sales support   N/A 1 2 3 4 5 6 7 8 9 10

8. ABC's ability to innovate   N/A 1 2 3 4 5 6 7 8 9 10

9. Price   N/A 1 2 3 4 5 6 7 8 9 10

10. Lead times   N/A 1 2 3 4 5 6 7 8 9 10

Additional comments

SECTION B: PERFORMANCE

How to complete Section B

We'd now like to know how satisfied or dissatisfied you are with the performance of ABC. Again circle the number which best reflects your views. This time show your level of satisfaction or dissatisfaction.

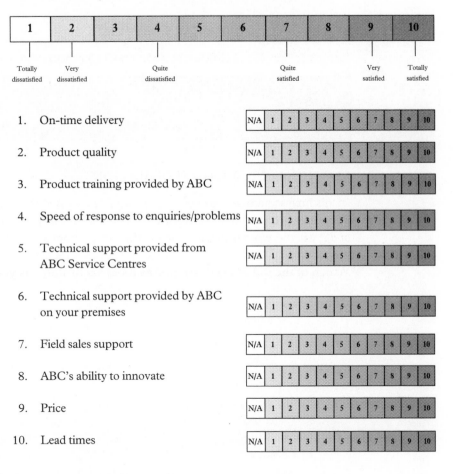

| 1 | 2 | 3 | 4 | 5 | 6 | 7 | 8 | 9 | 10 |

Totally dissatisfied | Very dissatisfied | Quite dissatisfied | Quite satisfied | Very satisfied | Totally satisfied

1. On-time delivery   N/A 1 2 3 4 5 6 7 8 9 10

2. Product quality   N/A 1 2 3 4 5 6 7 8 9 10

3. Product training provided by ABC   N/A 1 2 3 4 5 6 7 8 9 10

4. Speed of response to enquiries/problems   N/A 1 2 3 4 5 6 7 8 9 10

5. Technical support provided from ABC Service Centres   N/A 1 2 3 4 5 6 7 8 9 10

6. Technical support provided by ABC on your premises   N/A 1 2 3 4 5 6 7 8 9 10

7. Field sales support   N/A 1 2 3 4 5 6 7 8 9 10

8. ABC's ability to innovate   N/A 1 2 3 4 5 6 7 8 9 10

9. Price   N/A 1 2 3 4 5 6 7 8 9 10

10. Lead times   N/A 1 2 3 4 5 6 7 8 9 10

Additional comments

SECTION C: ABC SERVICE CENTRES

Please tick the appropriate box for the ABC centre that you have dealings with.

Birmingham ☐		Leeds ☐		Newcastle ☐
Bristol ☐		Manchester ☐		Southampton ☐

SECTION D: ADDITIONAL COMMENTS

Please use the space below for any additional comments about ABC.

SECTION E: GENERAL INFORMATION

In this final section, we ask you to give us a few details about yourself. This is important because different groups of customers often have different needs, and it will therefore help us to analyse the survey more accurately.

Which of the following descriptions most accurately fits your job?

General management ☐		Finance ☐		Customer service ☐
Purchasing ☐		Quality ☐		Sales ☐
Production ☐		Technical ☐		IT ☐

Other: _____

Which of the following business sectors is your organisation in?

Automotive ☐		Electronics ☐		Packaging ☐
Chemicals ☐		Engineering ☐		Plastics ☐
Computers ☐		Machine tools ☐	Telecommunications ☐

Other: _____

THANK YOU VERY MUCH FOR TAKING THE TIME TO COMPLETE THIS QUESTIONNAIRE. YOUR VIEWS ARE MUCH APPRECIATED

Please return your completed questionnaire using the envelope provided (or any other suitable envelope) to the following FREEPOST address: **The Leadership Factor Ltd, FREEPOST, Taylor Hill Mill, Huddersfield, HD4 6RS**

APPENDIX 2 TELEPHONE SURVEY QUESTIONNAIRE

ABC Ltd Customer Survey: Telephone

Classification data:

Interviewer: _____ Date: _____ Interview No: _____

To be completed by the interviewer before the interview
Please tick the appropriate boxes below:

Job function:

General management	☐	Finance	☐	Customer service	☐
Purchasing	☐	Quality	☐	Sales	☐
Production	☐	Technical	☐	IT	☐

Business sector:

Automotive	☐	Electronics	☐	Packaging	☐
Chemicals	☐	Engineering	☐	Plastics	☐
Computers	☐	Machine tools	☐	Telecommunications	☐

Other: _____

Account size:

Large ☐   Medium ☐   Small ☐

INTRODUCTION

Good morning/Good afternoon.

My name is Jim Alexander from The Leadership Factor and I'm calling on behalf of ABC. I understand that Mr Smith has written to you explaining that we have been asked to carry out a customer satisfaction survey on ABC's behalf. Did you receive the letter? . . .

Would it be convenient to spend 10 minutes answering a few questions now or would you prefer me to make an appointment for a more convenient time?

Could I assure you that in accordance with the Market Research Society code of conduct the information you provide will not be linked with your name unless you want it to be, but will be combined with other responses to provide information which will help ABC to fully understand and meet customers' needs.

I'd like to start by exploring the factors that are important to you when dealing with ABC.

What would you say is your most important requirement as a customer of ABC (Prompt: What is the main thing that ABC have to get right if you're going to be a satisfied customer?)

Requirement

So——is your single most important requirement as a customer of ABC. If you had to rate its importance to you by giving it a score out of 10, what score would you give it?

Score

SECTION A: IMPORTANCE

I'm now going to suggest a more detailed list of requirements and I'd like you to indicate how important or unimportant each one is to you by giving it a score out of 10, where 10 out of 10 would mean extremely important and 1 out of 10 would mean of no importance at all. When deciding your mark, you may find it helpful to compare the importance of the requirement in question with your number one requirement of (repeat the requirement).

1. On-time delivery ☐

2. Product quality ☐

3. Product training provided by ABC ☐

4. Speed of response to enquiries/problems ☐

5. Technical support provided from ABC Service Centres ☐

6. Technical support provided by ABC on your premises ☐

7. Field sales support ☐

8. ABC's ability to innovate ☐

9. Price ☐

10. Lead times ☐

Note any additional comments in the spaces below:

Item no.   Comments

SECTION B: PERFORMANCE

How to complete Section B

We'd now like to know how satisfied or dissatisfied you are with the performance of ABC. We would therefore like you to score how satisfied or dissatisfied you are with each of the items that we just covered by giving each a score out of 10 where 10 is totally satisfied with ABC's performance and 1 is totally dissatisfied.

1. On-time delivery ☐

2. Product quality ☐

3. Product training provided by ABC ☐

4. Speed of response to enquiries/problems ☐

5. Technical support provided from ABC Service Centres ☐

6. Technical support provided by ABC on your premises ☐

7. Field sales support ☐

8. ABC's ability to innovate ☐

9. Price ☐

10. Lead times ☐

If any item is scored 6 or lower probe reasons:

Item no.	Comments

SECTION C: ABC SERVICE CENTRES

Which ABC centre do you mainly deal with?

Birmingham	☐	Leeds	☐	Newcastle	☐
Bristol	☐	Manchester	☐	Southampton	☐

SECTION D: PRIORITIES FOR CHANGE

I would like you to imagine that you were the Chief Executive of ABC. What changes would you make? It might be helpful to think in terms of urgent, short-term changes and longer-term changes.

Short-term

Longer-term

SECTION E: ADDITIONAL COMMENTS

That's all the questions I have. Do you have any additional comments?

THANK YOU VERY MUCH FOR YOUR HELP. YOUR VIEWS ARE MUCH APPRECIATED

APPENDIX 3   INTERNAL SURVEY QUESTIONNAIRE

ABC Ltd Customer Service Questionnaire: Internal

INTRODUCTION AND GUIDANCE

ABC is currently undertaking a survey to measure the satisfaction of our customers. In order to help us make the most of the results we would like all ABC employees to fill in a very similar questionnaire to the one we sent to customers. Please answer the questions as honestly and as objectively as you can and return the questionnaire in the pre-paid envelope to our research agency, The Leadership Factor. The questionnaires are anonymous so no views will be traceable to any individual

Please return the questionnaire by **[date]**.

How to complete Section A

In this section, we would like you to score how important or unimportant you think the issues listed are to our customers.

Some issues may be more important than others so, first of all, read through all the questions before deciding which you think will typically be the most important requirement of our customers. Then score the level of importance out of 10 using the following scale.

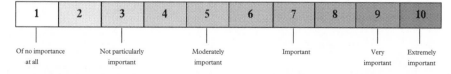

1	2	3	4	5	6	7	8	9	10

Of no importance at all — Not particularly important — Moderately important — Important — Very important — Extremely important

Score what you think will be customers' most important requirement first, then score the rest in that section.

For example, look at Question 1, 'On-time delivery'. If you think that 'On-time delivery is the most important requirement of customers, you should circle box number 10 as shown.

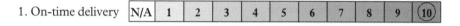

1. On-time delivery N/A | 1 | 2 | 3 | 4 | 5 | 6 | 7 | 8 | 9 | (10)

Then score the remaining items in the list using the same scale. If you feel that an issue is not relevant to customers, or you have no direct experience of what is being asked, you should tick the box marked 'N/A'.

SECTION A: IMPORTANCE

How important or unimportant do you think the following are to our customers?

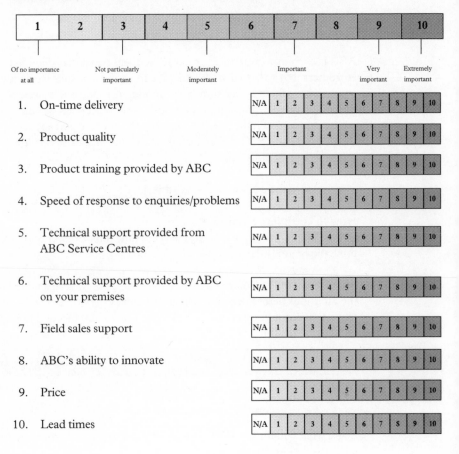

1. On-time delivery

2. Product quality

3. Product training provided by ABC

4. Speed of response to enquiries/problems

5. Technical support provided from ABC Service Centres

6. Technical support provided by ABC on your premises

7. Field sales support

8. ABC's ability to innovate

9. Price

10. Lead times

SECTION B: PERFORMANCE

How to complete Section B

We'd now like to know how satisfied or dissatisfied you think customers are with the performance of ABC. We would therefore like you to score ABC's performance on each of the items. Again circle the number which best reflects your views, but this time show how satisfied or dissatisfied you think customers are with ABC's performance.

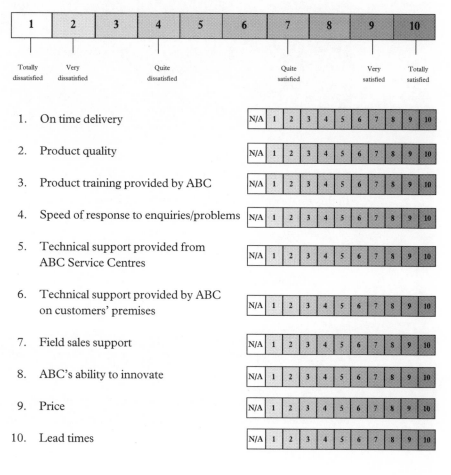

| 1 | 2 | 3 | 4 | 5 | 6 | 7 | 8 | 9 | 10 |

Totally dissatisfied — Very dissatisfied — Quite dissatisfied — Quite satisfied — Very satisfied — Totally satisfied

1. On time delivery   N/A 1 2 3 4 5 6 7 8 9 10

2. Product quality   N/A 1 2 3 4 5 6 7 8 9 10

3. Product training provided by ABC   N/A 1 2 3 4 5 6 7 8 9 10

4. Speed of response to enquiries/problems   N/A 1 2 3 4 5 6 7 8 9 10

5. Technical support provided from ABC Service Centres   N/A 1 2 3 4 5 6 7 8 9 10

6. Technical support provided by ABC on customers' premises   N/A 1 2 3 4 5 6 7 8 9 10

7. Field sales support   N/A 1 2 3 4 5 6 7 8 9 10

8. ABC's ability to innovate   N/A 1 2 3 4 5 6 7 8 9 10

9. Price   N/A 1 2 3 4 5 6 7 8 9 10

10. Lead times   N/A 1 2 3 4 5 6 7 8 9 10

SECTION C: ADDITIONAL COMMENTS

If you have any additional comments whatsoever regarding the service we provide to our customers, make use of the space below.

SECTION D: GENERAL INFORMATION

In this final section, we ask you to give us a few details about yourself. This is important because it will help us to analyse the survey more accurately

Which of the following ABC Centres are you based at?

Birmingham	☐	Leeds	☐	Newcastle	☐
Bristol	☐	Manchester	☐	Southampton	☐

THANK YOU VERY MUCH FOR TAKING THE TIME TO COMPLETE THIS QUESTIONNAIRE. YOUR VIEWS ARE MUCH APPRECIATED

Please return your completed questionnaire using the envelope provided (or any other suitable envelope) to the following FREEPOST address: **The Leadership Factor Ltd, FREEPOST, Taylor Hill Mill, Huddersfield, HD4 6RS**

APPENDIX 4:   *SATISFACTION BENCHMARK*

Many organisations conduct their own surveys to measure customer satisfaction, but to gain the full benefit from the exercise the results need to be compared with those achieved by other organisations. *Satisfaction Benchmark* is a service that aims to assist organisations to understand their relative performance and will:

- measure relative performance compared to all organisations as well as companies within a specific industry;
- compare scores for individual customer requirements to create relative performance ratings for individual product/service attributes;
- suggest realistic targets for customer satisfaction based on The Leadership Factor's experience in the field;
- provide feedback material to educate all levels of an organisation about the results and conclusions from a satisfaction survey;
- suggest improvements that can be made to methodology to create more reliable results.

Using a database of results from all the surveys that The Leadership Factor has conducted, any company's results can be placed in the *Satisfaction Benchmark* league table. This instantly demonstrates their relative position against all other organisations. Not only does this provide a measure of relative performance, but it also allows a company to measure its progress within an increasingly customer-aware environment. The average level of customer satisfaction will rise over the years, so to make real progress a company must improve further than other organisations. The database is continually being updated so that it reflects recent (and therefore valid) performance standards.

The second stage of benchmarking involves concentrating on individual requirements. Companies wish to know their overall position, but an organisation that prides itself on after-sales service, for example, may be interested to know exactly how they are seen to perform on after-sales service compared with other companies. This task should not necessarily be done simply within a company's industry. When customers consider their evaluation of the after-sales service they received when they bought a new car, they are unlikely to have had many similar experiences within the last few years. In practice, therefore, customers will make this judgement by comparing their experiences with the after-sales service they received when they bought their washing machine or computer.

As well as actually benchmarking your results, The Leadership Factor also uses its wealth of experience in the field of customer satisfaction measurement to evaluate the methodology that companies have used and suggests possible improvements that could be made to further the validity of their results.

Also provided is material that enables an organisation to feed back its results to all levels of staff throughout the company. This is crucial, as every member of staff who comes into contact with the customers, or whose job will ultimately affect customer satisfaction, must fully understand the survey results and their implications if they are to be motivated to improve customer satisfaction.

How does Satisfaction Benchmark work?

Organisations interested in benchmarking their customer satisfaction performance need to complete a simple application form to provide details of their results and the survey approach followed to obtain those results. It is necessary to understand the methodology to ensure that like is being compared with like when the results are benchmarked.

From the data an overall satisfaction index is calculated and entered along with the individual attribute scores on the *Satisfaction Benchmark* database. From this it is possible to compare both the overall index and the individual attribute scores against several hundred other results.

Naturally individual company results are not identified, as this would be a breach of confidentiality.

For more details of the service contact:

Ian Ralph, The Leadership Factor Ltd, Taylor Hill Mill, Huddersfield, HD4 6JA, UK
Tel: 01484 517575
Fax: 01484 517676

INDEX